Parents matter most, which is why the generation that has come of age since Stonewall often begins the process of coming out at home, in adolescence. What parents know matters most, which is why the generations that came of age before Stonewall often end the process of coming out at home, in middle age. This is not really the contradiction it seems, for the teenager anxious to share his self-discovery and the adult determined to spare his family that same discovery are both acknowledging the primacy of the parent-child relationship.

Thomas Garrett in the *New York Native*

PARENTS MATTER

*Parents' Relationships with
Lesbian Daughters and Gay Sons*

by Ann Muller

The Naiad Press, Inc.
1987

Printed in the United States of America
First Edition

Cover design by The Women's Graphic Center
Typesetting by Sandi Stancil

Chapter 9, now entitled "Why Parents Ask 'What Did We Do Wrong?' " appeared in a shortened and different version in *The Advocate*, Issue 392, April 17, 1984.

Acknowledgements: The author gratefully acknowledges the permission of Mitchell Beazley International to quote extensively from the work, *Sexual Preference, Its Development in Men and Women* by Alan P. Bell, Martin S. Weinberg, and Sue Kiefer Hammersmith, first published by Indiana University Press, Bloomington, Indiana, in 1981.

Library of Congress Cataloging-in-Publication Data

Muller, Ann, 1935—
    Parents matter.

    Bibliography: p.
    Includes index.
    1. Homosexuals—United States—Family relationships.
    2. Parent and child—United States.   I. Title.
HQ76.3.U5M85 1987   306.8'74   86-28490
ISBN 0-930044-91-6

To Frances Biscotto

and the memory of her son, Tommy

PARENTS MATTER

Parents' Relationships with
Lesbian Daughters and Gay Sons

CONTENTS

x

AUTHOR'S PREFACE

Most of the existing literature on homosexuality describes gay males. Lesbian experience is sometimes added on like the tail of a kite. This book is different. It draws evenly from the stories of lesbian daughters and gay sons. It was planned that way.

It is different in another way that was not planned. It shows, ever so consistently, that the daughters who contributed to the book had more difficulty getting along with their parents than did the sons. This is not to say it was easy for the sons and their parents. What it does say is that there were fewer positive daughter-parent relationships, and those relationships seemed to turn on different factors than the relationships of sons and parents.

My own relationship with a gay son provided the seed for this book. "Yeah," our son Jason told his dad and me in the winter of 1980, "I'm gay," as if it were an unimportant detail of the story he was telling. It was, of course, neither a detail nor unimportant. He said those words on that particular February afternoon because he was desperate. At nineteen, he had met, head-on, the hostility of a world that viewed him, wrongly, as perverted and sick.

At first I processed his disclosure through my own distress and maternal guilt. Later, I began to question those early feelings. Eventually, my doubts turned to a sort of quiet, dogged anger which came from the slowly recovering sense of myself as a good mother and my husband as a very fine father indeed.

Two things contributed to that anger. First, I read about homosexuality. Almost without exception, everything I found to read in those years was based on the Freudian theory that strong mothers and weak fathers cause a child who would otherwise be heterosexual to become homosexual. Second, I went to a support group for parents of lesbian daughters and gay sons. Within that group I met not only other parents who failed to fit the Freudian model but self-identified lesbians and gay men who challenged all the negative notions on homosexuality.

So it was that I came to write this book; I wished to better understand what happens in families like my own. I am not trained to do scientific research. Nor is my work the product of a clinically planned and controlled study. It is, instead, the result of observation, reading, simple arithmetical calculations, and the ideas and experiences of others.

Furthermore, most of the people who contributed to this book, including the author, live in the Chicago area. The information and conclusions presented here are, therefore, self-limiting and do not necessarily draw a larger picture. It is hoped, however, that this book will stimulate an interest in wider and more scientifically designed research on the relationships between parents and their gay offspring. Not much is known about these relationships aside from the self-fulfilling efforts of those who seek to "prove" that homosexuality is caused by bad parents.

My intent was not to assign blame but rather to see how parents absorbed the fact that a daughter or son was homosexual, and why it was that some parents were able to accept that fact more easily than others. To do that, I interviewed seventy-one people, sixty-one lesbians and gay men and ten parents. Just over half of them (52%) were daughters and parents of daughters; just less than half (48%) were sons and parents of sons. Seventeen percent of those I interviewed were black. Together, they told the stories of a hundred and eleven relationships between a parent and an adult child. I interviewed only those who had had a specific exchange that identified themselves as lesbian or gay with a parent, in other words, only people who were "out" to a parent. The parents I interviewed had had such an exchange with one, or in one case, with two of their children.

I chose to interview a majority of daughters and sons rather than parents for two reasons. First, I had met and talked to many parents during the years I was active in the parents' support group. I knew their stories as I knew my own. In contrast, at the time I started the work of this book, I knew little from the point of view of daughters and sons.

Second, I recognized that only a small number of parents come to parents' support groups compared to the large number who do not and that by doing so, by virtue of the single fact that we seek out such groups and do not remain isolated, we are atypical of most parents of gay offspring. I did, in fact, interview three parents from the group; I also met and interviewed seven other parents. My experience, however, was that most parents who had not been to the group, even when promised anonymity, were reluctant to talk about themselves as parents of lesbians or gay men. Furthermore, because of that reluctance on the part of so many parents, I have chosen to present all of the stories in this book anonymously.

I am, therefore, enormously grateful to the people who contributed to this book. Indeed, without them, there would be no book. Several provided support and assistance throughout the years of research and writing and became good friends in the process.

All of them, like me, wanted to better understand what had happened within their own families, and they hoped by telling their stories to increase the understanding of others.

Several other people including my family—Herman, Jason, Lori, and Tarif—made this book possible. Their names are Julia Rice, Paul Varnell, Ann Greene, Justine Kawalek, Carole Sherman, Georgie Walker, Jill Dilger, and Mary Borhek.

* * * * *

INTRODUCTION

Parents today are more likely than ever before to hear a daughter or son say the words, "I am a lesbian," or "I want you to know I'm gay." These words are being spoken because many are now unwilling to hide a same-sex orientation.

That new attitude is undoubtedly related to an event that happened almost twenty years ago. On a June night in the summer of 1969, a gay bar called the Stonewall Inn in New York City's Greenwich Village was raided by police. Police raids were common occurrences in gay bars in 1969. But, unexpectedly, that night the men in the bar fought back. They resisted arrest.

Their actions set in motion a social reform patterned after the civil rights movements of blacks and women. Lesbians and gay men began to challenge the laws and values of a society that assigned them second- or, perhaps more accurately, third-class status.

They continue that challenge today, and a vital aspect of their work is public identification of themselves as lesbians and gay men. Their candor has heightened the awareness of all gay women and men to both the risks and benefits of being open.

More and more are taking those risks with friends, colleagues, employees, and employers. More and more are coming out to parents, too.

Coming out is a phrase used throughout this book. It means the end of deception; it is the opposite of being closeted or hidden. People who recognize themselves as being erotically and emotionally attracted to the same sex rather than the opposite sex have come out to themselves. Those who share that information with their parents have come out to their parents. Parents, too, come out when they identify themselves as mother or father of a lesbian daughter or gay son.

Certain other words appear frequently in this book. And because they do not have the same meaning to all people, their definitions, as I use them, follow.

- *Sexual orientation* is the integral, unchosen part of us all that responds erotically to another person. It is separate from our biological sex and our gender identity which is our sense of being either female or male. It is also separate from sex roles which are learned behaviors identifying the concepts of femininity and masculinity.
- *Same-sex orientation* refers to the sexual orientation of a lesbian or gay man.
- *Lover* identifies the partner or significant other person in a lesbian's or gay man's life. Some find the word "lover" distasteful, but "friend" devalues her or his importance, and the English language does not yet

contain words comparable to the heterosexual terms "wife" and "husband."

- *Homosexual* in its descriptive form identifies only a person's same-sex orientation. It never acknowledges a whole human being; therefore, it is not used here as a noun. *Homo,* incidentally, comes from the Greek root meaning sameness, not from the Latin root which means man.
- *Gay* as an adjective describes a whole person who works, laughs, eats, sleeps, and also loves someone of the same sex. It usually describes a male.
- *Lesbian* is used in the same wholistic way to describe a female; it also serves as a noun, as in, "My daughter is a lesbian."
- *Homophobia,* a term first used by psychologist George Weinberg, describes an irrational fear of either appearing to be homosexual or of being in close quarters with people who are homosexual. Homophobia in our society is evidenced by a large number of negative myths and stereotypes.

Finally, this book does not deal with the causes of same-sex orientation. Why some women and men are attracted to the same sex rather than the opposite sex is a subject that fascinates many, particularly newly-aware parents of gay offspring. This book, however, moves forward from a recognition that homosexuality exists, that it has been around for a long time, and that no one understands its cause or, more importantly, the cause of any of the varied expressions of human sexuality including heterosexuality. What is more, even if that information were available, it would not be necessarily helpful or even relevant to the relationships between an adult lesbian or gay man and her or his heterosexual parent. What *is* relevant is that the information of a same-sex orientation was exchanged and that it has had an impact on the relationship between adult child and parent.

* * * * *

CHAPTER 1

WHO WE ARE

A daughter and her mother weave together their memories of a Saturday that neither of them will ever forget. The daughter speaks first. . .

> Nobody believes me when I tell them this, but as I was driving to work that morning I thought about that very thing: If my folks would get a letter that said I was gay, how would I handle it?

The mother's story begins later that same morning. . .

> It was on a Saturday morning that my husband and I received it. The mother of our daughter's friend

wrote us a very nasty letter and that's how we found out. That person did not sign it. She printed it, but we just knew who it was from.

> When I came home from work, my mother told me that she and my father wanted to talk to me after I was done with my ballet class. I could tell from her tone that this was going to be serious. I did terrible at dancing. . . .

I talked to her. Her father didn't talk. I said to her that we had received this letter, and I let her read it.

> It was a good page long, saying how sleazy I was, that I was sick and disgusting. I was feeling really angry. I looked up at my parents and said, "Are you asking me something or do you just want me to read this?" They said, "Well, is it true?"

> "The only thing that's true in this letter is that I'm a lesbian. The rest of it is garbage."

Six years later:

> We don't talk about it. I mean, it's there. She is and that's all there is to it. It's the same as it was before I knew she was gay. It's just given me one more thing to worry about. That's all.

> Initially I think our relationship was a little worse. Then I think it got better because I

started to feel more comfortable with talking about what I was doing. I think they got to know me better, know me more.

A son describes what happened when he went home to tell his mother and father he was gay.

> I stalled and stalled and stalled and then realized that I was pushed up like within a half hour of my grandparents arriving for dinner. In retrospect, I should have put it off, but I thought, No, let's go ahead.
>
> I asked them to come in the kitchen, and I told them maybe they'd better sit down. My mother immediately got nervous. Her first reaction was, "Do you need money?" I said, "No." Then I said, "Well, I always need money, but that's not what I'm telling you." Her second reaction was, "You got some girl pregnant." At that point I was so nervous, I started laughing. . . . My next statement was, "I'm gay."
>
> As soon as I'd said it, I realized, Well, that's it. You've done it all now. I didn't do any of the leading up I had planned. I didn't lay any groundwork. It just came out.
>
> We spent the next half hour talking, and it was mostly me doing the talking. I finally said, "Will one of you please say something?" My dad was the first one to speak, and he said, "When did you first decide you were a

homosexual?" My mother turned to him and said, "Well, Jesus Christ, Tom, when did you first decide you were a heterosexual?"

From that point on, my mother took the role of Why-did-you-tell-your-father? He'll-never-be-able-to-handle-this. She and I sat later that evening after my grandparents left and talked for a long time. She cried at that point, telling me that her biggest concerns were that she wasn't there to help me through the difficult process of coming out and that my father couldn't handle this.

I remember all of that very distinctly, because it was several years later that I came to understand that my father was the one who had no difficulty with it. I can't say he accepted it. What he did was say, Fine, I don't like that aspect of you, but I'll just set it over here because I love you, and I want this relationship with you to continue.

My mother, as it turns out, had a much more difficult time dealing with it; ninety-nine percent of her liberalism was fine for other people but not for me.

Eight years later:

If my father is calling to invite me to a family function, he's always been good about including whoever I am living with at that time, but beyond that [my being gay] really doesn't get talked about a great deal. My mother and I talk about it much more frequently, but now it is generally talked about in terms of her dealing with it.

Parents' responses to the disclosure that a child is homosexual are almost always profound. Many feel like a bomb has dropped on them. Some wage a counter attack. Others, like the father above, make a leap of love which maintains the family connection without acknowledging the coming-out message. Most parents respond out of a confusion of denial and concern, guilt and love. The expression of those contradictions mark the beginning of a new relationship between parent and child.

That relationship and the things that shape it are the subject of this book. Seventy-one men and women, half lesbians and parents of lesbian daughters and half gay men and parents of gay sons, described their experiences within that relationship. From their stories came new insights. For instance . . .

- Early parent-child relationships did not always predict how well parents and their adult gay offspring got along.
- Whether or not parents attended church or other religious services regularly seemed to have no connection to the relationships.
- Being an only child or one of two children had a negative impact on daughters' relationships with parents, but the same situations were positive in the relationships of sons and parents.

In addition, this book identifies two previously unrecognized sources of trouble.

6

- Homophobic sex-role expectations fostered a push-me-pull-me dynamic in many families as the children were growing up, and later those same expectations shaped very different relationships in the families of lesbian daughters than they did in the families of gay sons.
- Freudian and neo-Freudian theories communicated an astoundingly negative message that was uniquely personal to the parents of lesbian and gay offspring. New research and a new perspective challenge those old ideas and offer parents an opportunity to reject the guilt created by them.

Finally, daughters, sons, and parents share the long-term effects of coming out to parents: how they got along five years after the disclosure; what happened when a parent said, "Don't come home again"; and why some parents were able to grow beyond acceptance to an increased closeness with their daughter or son.

To say it another way, coming out to parents was a risk. As one daughter put it, "If I come out to a friend and she rejects me, well, I have other friends; I will always find other friends. But I will never find other parents." Why, then, take that risk? Daughters and sons answer that question.

> (D)* It's kind of an approval thing. I would like the word from my parents, particularly my mother, that I'm okay in my entirety, that everything about me is okay, not just when I tell her the things she wants to hear.

* * * * *

---

*(D) = daughter; (S) = son; (mD), (fD) = mother or father of daughter; (mS), (fS) = mother or father of son.

(D)   For a long time I thought I could be open in general to the world if only my parents knew, if I could somehow let them know. If I could have a good relationship with them, it wouldn't matter what the rest of the world thought.

* * * * *

(S)   I thought I'd never be physically well until I dealt with this.

* * * * *

(S)   Leonard Matlovich said at the Mattachine Society here in Chicago several years ago that he woke up one morning and realized he'd lived half his life for his parents' neighbors. I think that's very sad.

The deep-felt desire human beings have for parental approval is coupled in the lesbian daughter and gay son with an equally strong desire to be honest about themselves within the primary parent-child relationship. Despite the risks involved, those combined needs often result in the decision to come out to a parent.

Ideally, that act offers benefits to both adult child and parent. Ann Greene, counselor therapist, educator, and mother of a gay son, believes coming out to parents has three advantages.

First and foremost, I think it is personally liberating for the gay person himself. There

is just no comparison, it seems to me, of
what it's like for a person to not be con-
stricted. Then there is the possibility of the
improved quality of the relationship between
the parent and the gay person. I can attest
to the fact that the honesty, the depth, and
the increased love and supportiveness are
extremely enriching. Then, thirdly, from the
parents' viewpoint, there is a unique and
wonderful opportunity to grow, to broaden
our consciousness, to feel, experience, and
understand a child as we might never have
done before.[1]

The experience of others confirms the possibility of such
an ideal resolution, but it also suggests caution.

(S)   I think that generally the notion of
coming out to parents is very good.
People think in terms of knocking things
down, closing out, instead of understanding that they've really opened
avenues.

* * * * *

(S)   I don't think you can have an honest
relationship with your parents, with
anyone significant in your life, if they
don't know something real fundamental
about your life, and your sexual identity
is certainly a very fundamental part of
you.

* * * * *

(D)   I don't think that you can have a good and complete relationship with your parents when some portion of your life is hidden away and never talked about. Now, heterosexual adults do not talk about *sex* with their parents, but they certainly talk about their spouses and their love affairs and their breakups.

* * * * *

(S)   I think it's a very good idea. You're only cheating yourself when you don't, and it's a burden whether someone wants to acknowledge it or not. It's a burden that the gay person has to carry around with them.

* * * * *

(D)   I think it's important to be open with your family cause if you can't come home, where can you go? Maybe that's just my conditioning, but that's what I've always been told. If you know your parents, if you've had an honest relationship, then I'd say go ahead and trust that relationship.

* * * * *

(mD) For myself, I find it's much nicer to know what's going on. No matter what is going on, I want to know what it is.

* * * * *

10

(D) I would ask myself what do I want to happen from this? Why do I want to tell them? I think you ought to take a look at why you're doing it, because you may have some expectations built in that will never materialize.

* * * * *

(fS) I think it would be up to the person himself to know his parents, what their feelings are going to be. I know that none of them are going to take it and say, "So what?" I don't think any parent will say that. Other people will say, "So what?" but when it comes to home, it's a different situation.

* * * * *

(D) I think it's a good idea if you're independent of your parents. If you are still financially dependent, I don't think coming out is a good idea. I think it can be postponed until you're independent.

* * * * *

(mD) Too many parents cannot deal with this, and without more educating by the churches, the schools, etc., it's a matter of how each family interacts.

* * * * *

(D)   A friend of mine is from a family where both parents are alcoholics, and they're constantly at war with one another. Consequently, their children are just side parts of their life. I think in a family situation like that, maybe it's best not to tell them. If they're not concerned about you on any level, why involve them in the most intimate thing in your life?

* * * * *

(S)   I sincerely believe a lot of people, a lot of parents, realize it and would rather not talk about it. So, therefore, there's no value in talking about it.

The dilemma of whether to tell or not tell parents is relatively new. The majority of gay men and lesbians over forty probably have not done so. "To the older generation," confirms psychologist George Weinberg, "telling parents seems out of the question."[2]

Author May Sarton first wrote openly of lesbianism when she was in her fifties. "I am well aware," she admits, "that I probably could not have 'leveled' as I did in that book had I had any family (my parents were dead when I wrote it). . . ."[3] The late Howard Brown, M.D., told a similar story.

I did not tell my parents that I was homosexual. Nor did most homosexual men of my generation tell their parents. We excused our reticence with the thought that we were sparing them the agony of having to think

> about us as sexual beings—or, to put it another way, of having to understand us. . . . Instead, we shared with them a version of our lives from which all the essential passages had been expurgated.[4]

Today, however, many daughters and sons of all ages are coming out to their parents. Exactly how many parents hear this disclosure is not known for sure, but these facts suggest it is not a small number.

- Based on the Alfred Kinsey studies of sexual behavior which found that ten percent of the population is wholly or predominantly homosexual, there are over 20 million gay men and lesbians in the U.S.[5]
- Because of the indisputable, if seldom considered, fact that every lesbian and gay man has, or had, a mother and a father, there are approximately 40 million parents of lesbians and gays in the U.S.
- Research shows that approximately half the parents from the samples studied knew of the same-sex orientation of their offspring.[6] While it is impossible to accurately project those figures onto the larger number of 40 million, it seems nevertheless clear that literally millions of parents not only have, but are aware they have, a lesbian daughter or gay son.

Despite the numbers, little accurate information is known about these families. Homosexuality in families has traditionally been hidden, and even today most parents of lesbian daughters and gay sons remain invisible. That one characteristic was common to nearly all the mothers and fathers described in this book. They hugged the information of their child's same-sex orientation close, keeping it secret.

When their children came out of the closet, it was almost as if the parents had replaced them in the dark.

(D) *Four years after the disclosure* Neither of my parents have told anyone.

* * * * *

(D) *After five years* My father may have discussed it with his sister who's the mother of a lesbian too . . . maybe. And then, again, very possibly maybe not.

* * * * *

(D) *After nineteen years* When I was active in gay lib, I scared my parents cause I was so open and political and out. My name was everywhere. In fact, a number of times I almost went on TV, and I worried my father to death with his keep-it-in-the-house attitude.

* * * * *

(S) *After two years* I have a gay cousin. I know about him; he knows about me. My parents know about me, and my parents know about my cousin and about my cousin's parents. My cousin knows about me, and my cousin knows about my parents knowing. My cousin's parents know, and my cousin's parents know about me and my parents. But

> nobody ever talks about it except me
> and my cousin.

* * * * *

(S)　*After eleven years* I am positive she has
never told anyone, anyone.

* * * * *

(S)　*After two years* I'm sure she's scared
they will laugh or maybe not say anything but make jokes. . . .

Invisibility, however, neither precludes the existence of these parents nor identifies them as a new phenomenon. Parents of gay sons and daughters have existed, like homosexuality itself, throughout history in a variety of cultures. The oral history of these parents and children dies with each generation. It is not handed down in the traditional way for two reasons: The parents are not talking about it, and their gay children rarely become parents of gay children. The written history of these families, with the exception of information drawn from psychiatric patients, is only slightly less obscure. Not until 1977 did a nonfiction book appear about parents and their mentally healthy, adult gay sons and daughters.[7] Even today there is only a handful of such books. Consequently the one family in four with a gay member brings little understanding and much negative information to the new reality in their lives.[8]

This book speaks from life experience to those millions of isolated parents and to the parents of tomorrow who will hear a child say, "I am gay," or "I am a lesbian." It speaks as well to the sons and daughters who said those words, to the ones who think of saying them, and to others who care about these families.

* * * * *

Getting ready to tell your father.

Carlucci, Carlo. *He Ain't Heavy, He's My Lover.* (San Francisco: Alternate Publishing, 1983.) Reprinted with the permission of the artist, Carlo Carlucci, and Alternate Publishing.

CHAPTER 2

TELLING PARENTS

I consider it a big step forward that, more often than in earlier times, homosexuals tell their relatives about themselves. . . it is far better to be open. . . .

Dr. Magnus Hirschfeld, 1914

Nothing matters as much to any of us as coming out to our parents. There is nothing as historic as reaching out to our parents and having them reach out to us.

Virginia Apuzzo, 1983

Coming out to parents is not, as one daughter said, "a one-incident thing. It's a process." The disclosure, however, begins that process.

Most of the daughters and sons in this book had thought about, agonized over, and sometimes even rehearsed coming out to their parents. Some of their disclosures took place according to plan. Some did not. All of them, however, were set in motion by something that might be called a catalyst.

The Catalyst

The catalyst for coming out to parents is distinct from the plan itself; it is the spur that makes the disclosure happen. Most of the disclosures occurred because one of three things happened: parents and children who did not see one another regularly got together for a visit, the son or daughter established or ended a relationship with a lover, or, a parent asked.

When distance separated family members, the disclosure was often planned to take place during a visit.

(D)   I told my family I was coming home. They knew it was odd for me to come home for only four or five days since it takes me like eighteen hours to drive home, but I thought, I'm ready to go home and drop a bomb on them and how dare I waltz off back to Chicago knowing how they're going to feel about this.

* * * * *

(D)   I think I set it up so they would ask me because by Labor Day of that year they told me they wanted to come up and see me in Chicago because they wanted to talk to me. They were staying with me for the night, and we were all in my apartment.

* * * * *

(mD) We had just come back from a family vacation in California, and she was leaving that afternoon to go back to Cleveland. I could sense an urgency, you know, I-want-to-talk-to-you, so, we came out in the kitchen. My heart was beating because I knew it was coming, and it was one of those things I didn't want to hear.

* * * * *

(mD) It happened in the airport, after Christmas vacation as a family, and she was catching a connecting flight back to her place of residence. I left the other family members in the car and walked her to the gate. I said, "This is a crazy time and place to talk, but I don't know when I'll actually see you again. . . ."

* * * * *

(S) When you start coming out, it just starts rolling along. I started sharing it with people and that sort of prepared me for a visit that I had in the context of a class trip to take time out and visit my family and lay a rather heavy thing on my mother.

* * * * *

(S) I went home for vacation on the 4th of July. I wanted to do it then because I usually only see them once a year and that's at Christmas, and I just didn't want to take the risk of having to deal with this along with Christmas.

* * * * *

(S) I was living with a lover at the time and about once a month my mother would come and spend the weekend with us. We had a very small apartment with one bed in the bedroom. From my point of view, she *had* to have known, although we'd never discussed it. Then one weekend she came, and I talked to her.

The relationship with a lover, either its excitement or its pain, was another common catalyst for coming out to parents.

(D) I was so wrapped up in my career that I never even thought much about anything so far as relationships. But one day I fell in love, and it just happened to be a woman. I thought, "Oh, God, not this too. I'm black. I'm a woman. I'm working in a man's world, and I'm lefthanded. What else do I need?" About four months later, we decided to live together, and that next morning I picked up the phone and called my mom.

* * * * *

(mD) She called up one day, hysterical and crying. She said, "I'm in love with my roommate." I said, "What's wrong with that?" and she answered, "She's a woman."

* * * * *

(D) I thought she was real neat. I mean she made an impression on me. When I got home I wrote on the blackboard all the different ways to write "woman"—the Es knocked out and the Ys put in or an O or an I or the Ms doubled. Then I told Mom.

* * * * *

(S) When I came out, I sort of burned the closet down around me. I didn't walk through the door. It just sort of exploded, and I walked right into my first relationship. I thought at the time that I was very much in love and very happy, and I wanted to share it with my mother.

* * * * *

(S)   When I was twenty-five I fell in love, and there developed a difficulty in that I didn't want to be away from him at Easter and Christmas. I wanted my parents to understand it had nothing to do with my love for them that I wasn't coming home. It was my love for him. So that was my decision to come home and talk to them.

* * * * *

(S)   I was involved in a relationship at the time. A few weeks before there had been Thanksgiving dinner. I had been invited to Thanksgiving dinner by my aunt and uncle and told that I was welcome, but my friend was not because my friend was not family. I thought it was important to tell my parents that I considered my friend as much family if not more so than my aunt and uncle and as much as themselves and why all of that was the truth.

Most of the daughters and sons had expected to initiate their disclosures to their parents, but in a large number of families a parent brought it up first in the form of a question. Mothers asked more often than fathers, and in some families the mother had brought up the subject more than once.

(D)   My mom didn't like the woman I was involved with, and she'd ask me questions like, "Why do I have to be so nice to this person?" I never wanted to get into it on the telephone, and I would say, "Oh, well, someday I'll sit down and explain it to you, Mom." Then when I was living at home in the summer, we were sitting around the kitchen table one night, and she said, "Well, what is it? Why does she have such a hold on you?" I just kind of stopped. . . I had thought about this for so long, and I didn't know what I was supposed to say.

* * * * *

(D)   I was home from work one day, and my father called. He wanted to know what I was doing home from work, and I got very irritated with the question. We had words, my father and I, and he gave the phone to my mother. They kept after me. This was not the only occasion that this had happened on the phone, and I had just had it. She pushed and pushed. Finally I said, "Mom, I think you know what it is, and I don't want to upset you. I'd prefer not to talk about it." She didn't say anything for a long time.

* * * * *

(D)   We were sitting at dinner at a local, casual restaurant, and we started . . . I don't know how it came up, but they

started talking about this cousin of
mine, my father's brother's son. We
have always suspected that he might be
gay. His name came up, and my mother
said, "I'm wondering . . . I'm wondering
about you. Are you a lesbian?" Just
out of the blue. I wanted to fall through
the floor, because I was totally not
prepared at that moment to talk about
it.

* * * * *

(S)   My freshman year down at school my
mother had asked me twice and then
on the third time is when it all came
out. It took me about three months to
figure out for myself, to really determine
for myself that I was gay, and so when
she'd asked me the two times before, I
only told her I didn't know.

* * * * *

(S)   One day my mother just said, "I want
to talk to you." She took me downstairs
where they have a little area fixed up
in the basement. I think she thought it
was going to be the most private there
because, of course, I had my younger
brother and sisters running in and
out. . . . Then she said, "I know that
you're going to gay bars. I know that

the friends you hang around with now are gay."

* * * * *

(S)   My mother had company over playing cards, and my mother's girlfriend initiated it. It was this friend of mine . . . he was a cheerleader at school, and he was a bit effem. He had these huge bell bottoms on, and he was walking through the house with his baton. One of my mother's girlfriends said, "Is that a sissy you're with? Is that boy a sissy?" I just laughed at her, and then my mother said, "Are *you*?" I said, "No, I'm gay," and she said, "What's gay?"

Some of the disclosures happened as the result of unusual circumstances.

(D)   Approximately two years after I had been divorced and was leading an active lesbian life, there was a large play, a lesbian play, that was written by a local woman. I was *in* the play. My family (to include eighteen members) was all coming to see me in this play. I knew in an audience of about five- to six-hundred people that the majority of them would be lesbians, and I wanted to give an ice breaker to my mother.

* * * * *

(D)   There were two different things. One was my sister was getting married, and I was going home for the wedding. Two, my lover, Marsha, was expecting a baby. Marsha couldn't come to my sister's wedding because of work obligations, and it was very important to me not to show up next time on my father's doorstep and say, "Hi, remember Marsha? Now we're three." For that reason, I wanted to verbalize it when I was home, so my father would not go, "Oh, my God, what's this child doing here? You never said anything to me."

* * * * *

(mS)   I have an old trunk upstairs, and I had some plants on it. I noticed that there was dirt on the floor and on top of the trunk, and I thought, why is this dirt around? So I opened the trunk, and I saw all these letters stuck in there. I'd never seen them before, and out of curiosity I opened the letters. They were written by another man to my son. They were love letters.

* * * * *

(S)   I wanted to tell her when I was in the hospital because I guess I thought I might not live. It ended up that I left the hospital five days later. She picked

me up at the hospital, and we went to
lunch. For some reason I couldn't wait
any longer.

Whatever the catalyst for coming out to parents and whether the disclosure was planned or accidental, the information still needed to be communicated. That communication also occurred in a variety of ways.

The Words Used

The mother who responded to her son's declaration by asking, "What's gay?" was not the only parent who failed to understand the word "gay" when it was first spoken. Yet, in contrast, another mother understood that her daughter was a lesbian from the oblique communication, "Janice is moving in with me." The language of the disclosures was as diverse as the families themselves.

Undoubtedly one explanation for such diversity of language is that sex is an uneasy subject between parents and children, one that becomes increasingly uncomfortable as the children grow up. "In most families," according to a recent review of the subject, "parents and children do not talk much about sex [and] when children grow old enough for conversations that have implications for their own sexual behavior, most of the talk ceases."[1] That was certainly true in my own family; it was also true in the families described for this book. One of my interview questions was, "Did you and your folks talk openly about sex at home as you were growing up?" The answer was almost always no. One son who had fourteen sisters and brothers said, "Sex was almost a taboo subject." Then he thought for a minute and remarked, "That's odd considering how much sex my parents must have been having."

Not only, then, are most parents uncomfortable discussing sex with their children, but, according to psychologist Vivienne Cass, nearly all parents as well as their lesbian and gay children are "socialized by and into a society that is antihomosexual and heterosexual in its outlook. Heterosexuality and, in certain circumstances, asexuality are portrayed as the only acceptable outlets for sexual expression."[2] This, too, was confirmed by over half of the daughters and sons who could not remember their parents ever having mentioned homosexuality as they were growing up.

In short, the language of the disclosures forced acknowledgment by two generations of not only the sexuality but the homosexuality of a daughter or son. Both acknowledgments were unfamiliar, uncomfortable, and unwelcome. No wonder the choice of words came hard.

Daughters, in particular, struggled with words. One wished she had been "a little stronger, a little more politically correct: 'Mother, I'm a lesbian,' " but another daughter was satisfied that she had used the word "gay." "Lesbian," she said, "even today, is a word that I use usually with other lesbians only. It's a word with a lot of meaning to a lot of people. It's a word that has meaning to me also, and it's not always positive." Some daughters, of course, did describe themselves as lesbians and others, both daughters and sons, avoided saying either "lesbian" or "gay."

Probably another reason the language of the disclosures varied so is because communication between family members, especially between parents and children, is often a familiar, nonverbal kind of shorthand that comes from the long intimacy of shared experiences. Communication within that relationship by tone, gesture, and expression was, after all, perfected in the early years before the child could speak. One daughter acknowledged that she and her mother "talk in circles a lot," and she illustrated that when coming out to her mother by asking, "We don't really have to talk about this, do we?" Her mother's answer was, "No, I know."

Others communicated the disclosures like this.

(D)   I'm involved in a relationship with her, and it's more than a friendship.

* * * * *

(D)   I'm a lesbian, and I want you to know about that.

* * * * *

(D)   I'll have you know that *I'm* one of those.

* * * * *

(D)   No, *she's* not black. What I'm telling you is I'm gay.

* * * * *

(D)   I think I will probably go to women and never be with men again.

* * * * *

(S)   The reason why I've been driving so much is I'm gay.

* * * * *

(S)   Bill is more than just a friend.

* * * * *

(S)   A friend of mine has this problem, and he needs to talk to his mother about it.

* * * * *

(S)   I'm homosexual. I've known this for a long time.

* * * * *

(mS) Are you heterosexual, heterosexual with homosexual tendencies, bisexual, homosexual with heterosexual tendencies, or homosexual?

* * * * *

(S)   I think I'm bisexual; I think I'm gay.

* * * * *

(mS) Are you okay?

* * * * *

(S)   The reason is that there's no one I want to be with more than Robert and there's no one Robert wants to be with more than me.

The words that were used, however, became important as the work of this book progressed, for only individuals who had specifically identified themselves as lesbian or gay to a parent and only parents who had heard that disclosure from a daughter or son were sought for interviews. This standard no doubt eliminated a majority of parents and offspring; it eliminated those who only tacitly acknowledge a same-sex orientation within their families.

It was more difficult than I first expected to make a distinction between disclosures that resulted from a specific exchange of information and those that did not. The example given above of the daughter who said, "Janice is moving in with me," illustrates the problem. In the end, with one exception, which will be highlighted later, the decision of whether or not a story was included was based on a combination of the words exchanged and the parent's reaction to that exchange.

For if the words of the disclosures provided a certain drama, the parents' first reactions to those words were often equally dramatic if not more so.

* * * * *

The storm before the calm. . . .

CHAPTER 3

Parents' First Reactions

Mom doesn't seem to care particularly, [Max] said, turning from the window, Why do you?

Because! His father brayed the word. I just don't like it, that's all. Why should I? Who the hell does?

Let's not drag the world into this, Pop, Max said, trying to be as light as possible.

The world is the point, John said. Is *everybody* wrong?

Yes! Everybody's wrong! Max shouted back. And it's not the first time.

From *The Family of Max Desir*
by Robert Ferro

Parents' first reactions are certainly colored by what they know or do not know at the time of the disclosure. Most of us, like the father above who could only say he objected "Because!," respond out of an abysmal lack of information and understanding. My own background illustrates the point.

The year I was thirteen, Alfred Kinsey published his controversial figures on male homosexuality. I certainly did not read Kinsey then; all I knew at thirteen was that anyone who wore purple to school on Thursday was *Queer.*

When I was eighteen, groups such as the Mattachine Society and the Daughters of Bilitis were being formed on the West Coast. I was getting married that year in Battle Creek, Michigan.

The year of the Stonewall Riots in New York City, 1969, I was busy raising children in a small Indiana town where I suspected I knew a *Homosexual.* He cut my hair.

Three years later, unbeknownst to me, another mother named Jeanne Manford carried a sign in New York City's gay parade that read, "Parents of Gays Unite in Support of Our Children." I lived in a Chicago suburb that summer; my son Jason was nearly thirteen years old.

Six years later, when he was nineteen, Jason said, in the manner of an aside, "Yeah, I'm gay." And with those three words I was thrust into an unfamiliar world.

It was, for all I knew then, a dangerous and evil world, not one in which I wanted my son to live. Nor was it a world I wanted to know.

My first response to Jason's statement came out of that ignorance, that cocoon of heterosexuality. It also came from a recognition of Jason's obvious, if not directly expressed need for support in what had been the traumatic ending of his first sexual relationship with another man.

He and I did not, however, discuss those events; we talked instead of his future plans, his wish to change schools. It was only later after Jason's father came into the room that our discussion centered on the disclosure. Herman was the one to ask, "Are you sure?" and "Have you tried other kinds of sex?" We all cried during that long afternoon.

I remember saying, "Jay, you'll be more discriminated against than I am as a woman." He answered, "Yes, that's true," and we hugged each other.

Parents bring, as I did, not only ignorance to the disclosure but our own individual strategies for handling stressful situations. Those strategies can vary from unconsciously rigid distortions of the truth to consciously adaptive ways of coping with the reality. For instance, Jason's dad who sought answers by asking direct, non-angry questions was coping more realistically with the disclosure than were Jason and I who initially skirted the subject.

More than a few daughters and sons were familiar enough with their parents' response to stressful family situations to accurately predict how their parents would react to the disclosure. For example, one daughter said, "It was complete uproar. I expected that and that is why I didn't tell them for a long time." Another daughter said, "My father rarely surprises me with his reactions." In several families, parents' responses mirrored their earlier responses to an unmarried daughter's pregnancy.

Overall, most parents' emotions ran high at first. Hostility, when it existed, seemed to be expressed early. Indeed, a study by Karla Jay and Allen Young reported that the parents of their respondents had reacted more negatively than siblings, employers, or others.[1] Nearly all the parents described for this book had shown some combination of shock, guilt, and denial. Others responded out of love.

Hostility

About a quarter of the parents were hostile at first. Rejection, a subject we will look at in detail in a later chapter, was a common element of those hostile reactions.

(D) My mother was furious and we argued. She said something to me at one point to the effect of how can you displace your duty to look up some woman's cunt or pussy. I was amazed because I could count the times I've heard my mother say "damn." I also remember her saying that she would not speak to me again, that she would have no further contact with me.

* * * * *

(D) The day I told my parents they considered throwing me out. I remember sitting there hoping they could just hold on. I was counting the minutes. I asked my father, "Would you rather that I be as unhappy as I have been in trying to live a straight lifestyle or can you learn to accept the fact that I'm happy being a lesbian?" (That's the first time I'd said the word.) He said, "I think I'd rather you were unhappy and *normal*!" I can also remember my mother saying that she felt she would be far more comfortable dealing with the fact that I was terminally ill with cancer.

* * * * *

(S) My mom was crying and my dad says, "You may as well have pulled the trigger." She started beating on me and like pulling at my hair, and she threw herself against the sliding glass door.

* * * * *

(S)   My stepfather found the pictures and he showed them to my mom. What happened was I came up the driveway and they were going somewhere. She was sitting in the car, and I said, "Hi, Mom, where you going?" but she didn't speak. She just shot me this dirty look. Then I remember she went off, got hysterical. She started screaming at me about pictures and hugging and kissing men, and she said, "Get out of my house. Get out of my house."

Shock, Guilt, Denial

Most of the parents, however, were not angry. They reacted in a variety of ways that expressed shock, guilt, or denial. Even when parents suspected—and most of them, particularly the mothers, were not surprised—their suspicions did not seem to temper the initial reaction. Some were emotional, some quiet, and some had almost no reaction.

(D)   My father's thing was, "If you're going to do something, then you have to take responsibility," and the responsibility at that point was don't-let-your-mother-find-out.

* * * * *

(D)   My mother's first reaction was, "Don't
      tell your father. It'd kill him." She was
      devastated. She really was, and she just
      started crying. It totally shocked her.

* * * * *

(D)   My father said, "Oh, my God, we were
      afraid of this." Then they really went
      on to totally lose it. I mean that night
      they were not at all the parents I had
      known for twenty-three and a half years.
      They reverted to an image I have of
      conservative, prejudiced parents that I'd
      never seen before. They were both cry-
      ing. They told me that they thought it
      was abhorrent and disgusting, and they
      felt like I had just died.

* * * * *

(D)   Mother was very careful about her
      words. Quietly disapproving, I might
      add. Maybe not so much because I was
      gay, but because we were talking about
      sexuality. And I guess the religious
      implications she had for a long time
      said that the sadness of my being gay
      will be that she will not see me in
      heaven. That really is sad for her.

* * * * *

(D)   My parents were leaving for Oklahoma
      that evening, and Dad called me half

way through his trip back home to tell me that he had decided to give up alcohol, kind of a penance or a novena, as it were, in their religion, praying that I would change this course in my life and come out of it in one piece and not be gay. I said, "Well, okay, Dad. That's really something."

* * * * *

(S)   My mother told me right to my face that both my brother and I have been a major disappointment in their lives. I took that real hard.

* * * * *

(S)   She just got sick. Quite frankly, it's funny to me now, and I don't know if I'm exaggerating this story because it's so funny to me. But as I remember, we finished our talk which didn't last that long, and she lay down on the sofa and was sick for a week. See, if you know my mother, that makes sense, though. I mean, that's the way my mother handles emotional situations. Everything went physical on her.

* * * * *

(fS) It was just like somebody hit me in the face with a brick.

* * * * *

(S)   My mother didn't have any negative reaction at all. She was silently stunned, and she didn't react pretty much one way or the other except that she tried to be understanding. . . . Things seemed fine, but I found out later every time I was out all she did was cry. And it was not mild crying. I mean it was pretty serious stuff.

* * * * *

(S)   She said, "Have you always felt this way?" Then the following week I get this letter saying how deeply hurt she had been. She wished there was something she could do to make it different. "Whatever you do," she wrote, "don't let the family know."

And Love

Despite these illustrations, it is important to recognize that parents also have the potential to be the most loving recipients of a coming-out message. More than a small number of parents demonstrated that. They reacted out of concern for their child and made their first reaction a reaffirmation of their love.

(mD)   It was a relief it was finally out and, of course, my daughter asked me how I felt. All I could say was, "Right now I feel numb. I love you, and you are our child, and it'll be okay."

* * * * *

(D) At the very end before Mother got out of the car, for somebody who is basically undemonstrative, she hugged me and said, "I love you," which for my mother is going a long way.

* * * * *

(D) My dad's reaction was, "Do you think it's genetic or environmental?" and I said, "I don't think anybody knows, and I'm not sure it matters anyway." Then he said, "Well, okay. Is that all right with you?" and I said, "Yeah, yeah." "Okay, fine," he said, and that was the end of the conversation.

* * * * *

(D) My mother looked up at me, and she said, "Well, Janie, I love all the members of your softball team."

* * * * *

(mS) My immediate reaction was that I thought it took a lot of courage for a kid of eighteen to deal with that kind of serious issue honestly and to go about it with good sense, you know, being open to us, being honest about it. . . . So, for me, in many ways, it was a positive experience.

* * * * *

(S) My mother just had her arm around me. She was compassionate; it was sort of pity. And she said something like, "Of course it's not your fault."

* * * * *

(S) She ended it with words such as, you know, "I love you no matter what. I'm your mother, and I've always been extremely proud of you. I will remain proud of you. That doesn't change my opinion."

* * * * *

(S) She just hugged me and told me she still loved me, and it didn't matter. There was no hesitation on her part at all.

That first reaction of parents, then, concluded the first step of a process. Coming out to parents is something, according to journalist Thomas Garrett, that "cannot be resolved in a single stroke, in one perfectly phrased personal declaration or one carefully manipulated conversation. It is a lifelong process, and it begins at the beginning."[2] And out of that beginning a new relationship develops.

* * * * *

YOU KNOW DAMN WELL. MARTHA,
THIS "GAY" THING ISN'T FROM
MY SIDE OF THE FAMILY.

CHAPTER 4

HOW IT WORKED OUT

Family life! The United Nations is child's play compared to the tugs and splits and need to understand and forgive in any family. That's the truth, I am sure, but, like every hard truth, we all try to pretend it isn't true.

> May Sarton in *Kinds of Love*

What it is, you're taking the family, whatever state it's in at the time, and you're messing it up. It's like taking one of those blenders and mixing everything up, and the risk is whether you can put the pieces back together right.

> A daughter defines the risk
> of coming out to parents

Families put the pieces back together in different ways, and some took longer to do it than others. In time, though, the two generations, if they remained connected, worked out a way to get along. In so doing, they created new relationships.

One hundred and eleven such relationships were described in the interviews for this book. They had been evolving for varying lengths of time. One was only a month old; another had lasted twenty-seven years. The average length of time between the disclosures and the interviews was five years and ten months.

Surprisingly, though, a greater length of time did not seem to make much difference in the way the daughters and sons and their parents got along. Most parents showed their strongest reaction at the time of the disclosure. Some continued to be highly emotional for a year or more. The majority did not.

In fact, the interview stories consistently described a response from parents that changed little as the years went by. Even parents who had heard the disclosure within the previous year did not exhibit widely changing behavior; indeed, their actions were indistinguishable from those of parents who had known for years.

Parenthetically, it is important to remember that most of these observations of parents came from daughters and sons, and an argument could be made that the parents themselves might have told a different story. My experience, however, with the reluctance of parents to talk about themselves as parents of lesbian and gay offspring, as set forth in the Preface, and my further experience with many parents in a self-help group for parents support the view that parents' initial reactions are followed within a year, or two at the most, by a second level of response, and once there, few parents make significant progress to a more positive stance. This was found to be particularly true of parents of lesbian daughters. It was less true of parents of gay sons who did become somewhat more positive as their sons matured and became financially independent. That difference will be discussed more fully later, but the central truth of the matter is that the attitudes of most parents changed little over the years.

This is not to say that parents accommodate the knowledge of a child's same-sex orientation either easily or rapidly. I do not believe that is the case. What it does say is that most parents do not seem to move through any lengthy, linear progression of stages that result in increased understanding and acceptance.[1]

One father, for example, said,

> For that first month I didn't know how to handle it. All I wanted was to protect him from the world, to keep him under my thumb, know where he was. I thought it would all leave his system, and he would finally wake up and say, "Yeah, you're right, Dad, it was all something that was just going through my mind, a phase that I was going through." But as time went on, I could see that that's the way he is, and that's all there is to it. So the way I could cope with it, as I say, I would block it out of my mind, and I went on from there.

"Blocking it out" was, as we have seen, a significant part of parents' initial reactions. It was also a common thread running through all the interview stories regardless of the length of time since the disclosure. Parents continued to deny their offspring's same-sex orientation by clinging to the notion that it was just a phase, by avoiding the subject, by refusing to go to a parents' support group, by insisting their son's lover was just a good friend, and by giving their daughter's phone number to her old boyfriends.

I once waited in a receiving line to meet the mother of a young friend. Several years after he son had come out to her, she, together with some other family members, attended their first gay church service. My friend's mother had agreed to do so at her son's urging because he was about to leave the country for an extended period of time and also because he was delivering the sermon that night. When I finally reached her, I introduced myself as a friend of her son's and went on to say, "I'm also the mother of a gay son; in fact, our sons graduated from the same high school." She blanched and stood silent. After an awkward pause, she acknowledged me by saying, "I'd like you to meet my sister." "Ah, yes," said the sister, who had overheard our exchange, "and we think he's a good son, too."

Parents' denial could be considered a form of conditional love as in, "I love you, but don't talk to me about being gay." I think, however, the reality is less simplistic. It is conditional love and it is not. A number of things, as we shall see, affected the individual relationships. On the other hand, a clear cause-and-effect connection links parents' denial to their isolation. Parents who are in the closet with their daughter's or son's disclosure are isolated from other parents, other gay people, and relevant new information.

The truth is that heterosexual parents have little motivation to understand or accept homosexuality. Unlike their sons and daughters who are motivated by sexual energy to risk the disapproval of a heterosexual world, parents stop short. Some stubbornly dig in and defend themselves with the ever available dogma of homophobia. Most just fail to put much positive energy into being parents of gay offspring. The rewards are not obvious.

Furthermore, many parents, particularly those with traditional moral values, will always find certain aspects of gay culture, such as cross dressing and the concept of recreational sex, objectionable.

The parents in this book, however, found three ways to live with their daughter's or son's same-sex orientation. They exhibited a hostile recognition of it, they exhibited a loving, open recognition of it, or they denied it with varying degrees of negativity or positivity.

Those responses were the primary characteristics that identified four different types of relationships. Indeed, parents' attitudes set the tone for what happened after the disclosures while daughters and sons who inevitably held the edge of experience and information, were often passive contributors to the relationships.

Two of the four types of relationships were viewed as negative, two as positive.* Overall, there were more positive relationships than negative, but this was true only because nearly three-fourths of the parent-son relationships were positive. Parent-daughter relationships, on the other hand, were almost evenly divided between positive and negative, with the balance tipping to the negative side.

Four Different Relationships

Loving Denial was the name given to the largest group of relationships. It was one of the two positive relationships, and it described how just under half of the one hundred and eleven relationships in this book worked. More than half of the parents and sons and about forty percent of the parents and daughters interacted in this manner. Some of the parents were more accepting than others, but all remained closeted, usually within the immediate family,

---

*How this was done is described in Appendix B.

with the fact that they had a gay child. Their acceptance was limited, in most instances, to their own child; however, not infrequently it included the child's lover. The parents' acceptance was conditional in that little overt recognition of the child's sexual orientation was tolerated. Daughters and sons contributed to the denial by monitoring their words and actions while in the presence of their parents, and most of them were satisfied, some even more than satisfied, with their parents' level of acceptance.

A father, for example, had for years included his son's lover and gay friends in family activities, but at one holiday dinner when his son unthinkingly addressed his lover as "Hon," the father who was at the moment helping himself to salad, "dropped the salad tongs and started piling the salad on his plate with his hands."

Half of the Loving-Denial relationships had weathered a stormy period after the disclosure, but nearly all of them had been loving before the disclosure. Furthermore, within a short time after the disclosures, many of the parents in Loving-Denial relationships had done something described earlier as a leap of love. Leaps of love, which are much like philosophical or religious leaps of faith, lessen the painful dissonance of parents who believe their child is good but homosexuality is bad; they are based, as the following illustrations show, on denial of a daughter's or son's homosexuality.

(D) My mother acted like she accepted it, but her whole thing was she wouldn't talk about it. It was like we were all family [but] if anything at all came up, any little innuendo that showed I was gay, she'd just close off completely, change the subject. Just pass around it and find another way to say the same thing. She *treated* us like we were a couple, but she couldn't really accept it in her mind.

* * * * *

(D)   The first month I did notice a reaction. My father was just a little stand-offish, and then it just sort of went away. I think my father really denies the whole thing. I think he sees us as two very intelligent, nice ladies, sort of like spinsters, who just don't like men, and they're going to be companions and live their lives together, and isn't that nice?

* * * * *

(D)   Their way of dealing over the years has been, "We love you. That's the thing we want to leave it with. We love you. We haven't worked through this. We may never work through this. We don't approve of this, but we love you." And we've been at versions of that for seven years.

* * * * *

(S)   Her immediate reaction was acceptance . . . not a lot of talking about it, not a lot of dealing with it. I can't say she was positive or negative on the

> subject, but she was positive on me as a person.

* * * * *

(S)   My mother's first reaction was it was okay for me to be gay, but all the rest were these nasty druggies who slit people's throats and robbed people.

Again, many parents in Loving-Denial relationships had made a quick, positive move. Some did it on their own. Others did so after a single counseling session or a conversation with a minister or priest or after reading one of the excellent books now available for newly-aware parents.[2] Some parents, such as those described next, made no such move.

Hostile Recognition described five percent of the total relationships, the smallest and the most negative group. Six parents were extremely hostile. Their belligerence centered on the sexual orientation of their offspring, although in all four families the relationships between parents and children were bad even before the disclosures. Looking back, the daughters and sons felt their parents had either withheld appreciation and approval as they were growing up or had given it unevenly so that they had never been sure what to expect. Furthermore, alcoholism, neglect, or abuse or a combination of those three had been a part of the early lives of both daughters and one of the two sons.

Nonetheless, the parents' hostility was not always apparent immediately after the disclosure. In fact, on the evening of the disclosure, one daughter thought, "It went really well. When I left, I hugged my mother at the door. We were both crying, and I said, "You know, if I had two parents to pick, you two would be the ones I would want."

That sentiment was short-lived, however, because within months both parents testified in a court of law that their daughter's lesbianism made her an unfit mother of her two children. As a result of that testimony, legal custody of the children was given to their father. "My parents said they did it for the sake of the children," the daughter said, "but when it was all over, they never even bothered to be in touch with my children again."

Estrangement between the daughter and her parents followed the court hearing. Several years later, when the mother became seriously ill, communication was reopened, but at the time of the interview, the daughter had not seen either parent in two years.

Another daughter came out to her mother over the telephone. Their first conversation, according to the daughter, "covered in a very intellectual fashion not only the fact that I was gay and who I was but how I felt about my relationship with my mother over the years." During a second call a few nights later, however, both mother and daughter were angry. "My mother then said," the daughter remembered, "she'd put up with so much from me. She didn't know what she'd ever done to deserve me, that I was devil-seed in her womb, and I had a warped and twisted mind and was basically crazy. Then she said she didn't want to talk to me anymore." At the time of the interview, mother and daughter had not talked in three years.

One mother appeared more distressed than angry at the time of the disclosure, and during the years that followed she read the Bible to her young son, hung a religious symbol on the rear view mirror of his car, and later sent him a book "on how to be a correct Catholic." At the same time, she was also, according to her son, a passive participant in the father's promise "to give me hell until my eighteenth birthday because I gave them so much hell." That promise included physical, mental, and verbal assault, foster homes, and police arrest of the underage son's lover. There had been no communication between these family members for nearly a year at the time of the interview.

The last Hostile-Recognition relationship was between a son and mother. The son came out at twenty-three to his sister, her husband, and his mother because an acquaintance had threatened to tell the family he was "weird." The mother's first reaction was to summon the police. There followed a month of violence that included threats, beatings, abusive phone calls, and rejection. The relationship broke off completely. Many years later, with the help of a psychiatrist, the son attempted reconciliation with his mother, but at the time of the interview, they were again alienated.

These stories were the saddest. All ended in long-term separation. The four children had lived the ultimate horror stories that are invariably a part of all conversations about coming out to parents. In a later chapter, they will tell whether or not they regret having come out to their parents and how they coped with their parents' rejection.

Resentful Denial was the other group of negative relationships. About a third of all the relationships were in this group. Importantly, though, almost half of all the parent-daughter relationships were here while less than a quarter of the total number of parent-son relationships were based on a parent's resentful denial.

Unlike the parents in the Hostile-Recognition group, these parents preferred not to acknowledge their child's same-sex orientation. Quite a few of them never did. Those who did, did so infrequently and in a negative manner. As one daughter said four years after the disclosure, "They learned to tolerate it and make faces."

One mother repeatedly substituted the term "berserkie" for "gay," as in, "Are all your friends berserkie?" A father described his daughter's lover of fourteen years as "a

nothing" and added, "You *would* get involved with somebody who's a nothing." Another father did not bring up
the subject for years, but shortly before he died, he
expressed a wish that his family never be told about his
daughter's lesbianism.

The daughters and sons in these relationships were more
than observers of their parents' denial; they facilitated it.
One daughter acknowledged, "I protect her a lot. For
example, she doesn't know any of my friends are lesbians
or gay men and most of them are." Another said, "So long
as things are easy, I don't make any direct remarks." Eight
years after the disclosure, a son knew "exactly how much I
can say to my father. I know what shocks him and I know
what he can handle which isn't much. When we talk, it's
the way you would talk to someone at a party."

None of these parents changed their attitudes quickly in
the way so many Loving-Denial parents had with their leaps
of love, although about a quarter of the Resentful-Denial
relationships had improved since the disclosures. Just less
than half of the relationships seemed unchanged by the
disclosures, with family members getting along much as
they had before. About a third, though, and over five times
as many parent-daughter as parent-son relationships had
deteriorated since the disclosures. In those families, the
adult children thought their parents were less approving of
them than they had been before the disclosures. Many
described more tension and more arguments. Others noted
less frequent, less loving or less honest communication with
their parents than they believed they had once had. Nor
did things improve with time; the average time between
disclosure and interview in the families where the relationships had deteriorated was four and a half years.

All but one Resentful Denial family was still connected.
In that single instance, the daughter had chosen not to be
in contact with her mother, and they had been apart for

almost a year at the time of the interview. In two other families, the sons thought their relationships with their parents had improved after they moved away from home.

Loving Open was the name given to the most positive group of relationships. Two daughters, five sons, and four parents described the relationships in this group. They made up eleven percent of the total. Most were relationships between parents and sons; most of the parents were mothers.

All of the relationships had been loving before the disclosures. About half the daughters and sons thought their relationships had even improved since the disclosures. Three sons still lived with their parents.

Two things set these relationships apart: One, the parents in them exhibited little denial of the sexual orientation of their offspring, and, two, they were fairly open and positive with others about it. All of the parents had mentioned it (came out) to at least some of their relatives and friends. Four of them had identified themselves publicly by speaking as parents of lesbians and gay men. Three were active members of Chicago's support group for parents.

The initial reactions of all but one of these parents had been loving. The exception was a mother who found out at the same time that both of her sons were gay. She described her reaction as emotional, a combination of shock, anger, and pain, that lasted three years.

> Then I said to myself, "I've got two healthy boys that are becoming more and more successful financially. I wanted that for them. They know who they are. They're happy. . . ." I had to stop and think, "Now, if I'm going to become part of their lives, then I better stop this."

This mother was one of two mothers in the Loving-Open group who had become significantly more positive and open over time. The other such mother was described by her son who died fourteen months after the interview of complications resulting from Acquired Immune Deficiency Syndrome, or AIDS.

He had come out to his mother as a young man and had moved to Chicago from the East coast soon after. His relationship with his mother had remained loving, but for eighteen years they had both avoided acknowledging his homosexuality. "It wasn't hidden," the son said, "we just never really talked about it." He told how the impact of AIDS changed that.

> Things have been a lot better over the past two years. We've been able to talk about my being gay just more openly. I guess I sort of stopped trying to skirt it myself; I don't bother to protect her at all anymore.

> Part of that change was a result of the cancer [Kaposi's sarcoma]. At first, I just told her it was cancer. I thought she'd have enough to worry about without trying to figure out the AIDS bit too. She was very quiet on the phone. I can't remember her words, but it was something like, "We're just going to have to learn to live with this and work it out."

> Then last April *Newsweek* did a whole article on AIDS.[3] They had been out here and interviewed me and in the article was this picture of me and the dog. The magazine had actually been off the stands for a while

[before] somebody brought it to my mother's attention. Then she couldn't find a copy, so she called. I was afraid about what she'd do, how she'd react.

I briefed her a bit about it on the phone and then I sent her a copy of the *Newsweek* article and a copy of the letter that I had written in [Chicago's gay newspaper] to show her how I was approaching it and dealing with it. It was actually a fund-raising letter, a money pitch to start the AIDS Action Project here in Chicago. I also sent her a letter that somebody had sent me, a terrific letter that said I was a good role model, positive, something like that.

Her answer was to raise money. She works in a fur market, and she went to her boss whom I've known since I was a kid. She took my letters, the copy of the *Newsweek* thing, and she went to everybody she knew in the fur market. Her boss took it to all the people he knew. She wrote letters to all her family and friends. She raised $2,000!

So [laughing] that's what I was protecting her from! Instead of having a hysterical mother, she was just here in July and she was fine. Of course, she worries. . . .

At the end of her son's illness, this mother took indefinite leave from her job and came to Chicago to care for him. "She was," according to her late son's lover, "constant in her devotion to him." The obituary noted that, "On Friday, saying that he wanted to sleep, he lapsed into a coma and passed peacefully at 8 p.m. surrounded by [his lover], his mother . . . and sister. . . .[4]

Two other parents in this group had apparently recognized their son's same-sex orientation at an early age. They had also accepted it in a natural, easy fashion. Their story, told by their son, is the single example in this book of a relationship based on tacit recognition rather than a specific disclosure. It is included because it provides a sharp contrast to many of the other stories.

I didn't share anything in common with any of my siblings. I think my parents saw me as an interesting personality all to my own. I can't tell you exactly how they got to know I was gay. I just grew up with it, and I was never told that what I was doing was wrong.

From the time I was in eighth grade, I had a friend named Jake, and we were together all the time. He was a very special part of my life, and my family understood that. My mother would say, "These are my sons," and here's a black guy and a white guy.

Then when I was nineteen I thought I needed more experiences in my life, and I started ignoring poor Jake. I remember I had gone to the movies with him earlier one evening and then I was going to go out to the bars with another friend later. My mother was very upset. We argued, and I ended up moving away from home. I kind of left Jake.

Today my life is exclusively gay, and I talk to my mother about things that I do. My

father's like the traditional father, he doesn't
say much. [But] I take my friends and my
current lover home. In fact, I'd like to move
back home. My brothers and sisters are
gone, and I'd love to have my parents all to
myself.

The remaining relationships in this group were also
heartwarming. They included

- a stepfather who "took each of my mother's fears
  individually and dealt with them. He was magnifi-
  cent!"
- a mother who "loves it when I bring gay friends
  home."
- a father who "walked the entire deal" of Chicago's
  Gay and Lesbian Pride Parade despite a history of
  heart attack, two bypass surgeries, and 99° heat.
- a mother who visits her son in San Francisco every
  winter and "cooks up a storm" while she's there.
  "We had seventy-five men for dinner last year . . . and
  they just loved it!"

In short, Loving-Open relationships were the most
satisfactory. They were not, of course, completely har-
monious all of the time, but they were more open and
mutually appreciative than the other three kinds of relationships.

Mutual appreciation, in particular, was much less the
experience of daughters and parents than it was of sons and
parents. The overall greater positivity of sons' parents was
particularly evident in this most positive group where

relationships between parents and sons outnumbered those between parents and daughters three to one.

* * * * *

CHAPTER 5

A CLOSER LOOK:
DAUGHTERS' PARENTS AND SONS' PARENTS

Few problems we gay people face are as agonizing as our
relationships with our parents. Most of us love and wish to
be loved by our parents.

David B. Goldstein in *The Advocate,* 1975

How parents respond to the knowledge that one of
their own children is homosexual would seem to depend on
the individual parents themselves, their experiences with
life, the events that shaped their view of the world and
how they had responded to those events.

Consequently, ten factors were identified which might
be expected to affect parents and the relationships that
developed after the disclosures: religion, education, geo-
graphical origin, prejudice toward others, political views,

length of time since disclosure, age of parents and age of the child, the number of siblings the gay child has, and the early parent-child relationship.

In an attempt to find whether or not these factors did indeed affect the way parents and their gay offspring got along, the relationships described for this book were identified as either positive or negative (by the definitions in the previous chapter and Appendix B) and were then distributed according to the family's background or situation within each of the ten factors listed above. Parent-daughter relationships were counted separately from parent-son relationships. Each factor was two-sided. For instance, parents had either grown up in big cities or in small towns and rural areas.

The factors presented first are those researchers have found correlate, with some consistency, to people's attitudes toward homosexuality. Correlates have been established by studies made of various population samples, but almost none of the existing research has sought to make a connection between the factors studied and parents of lesbians and gay men. Some surprises occurred when that connection was made.

Religion

Religious teaching, particularly in the United States, is the primary social force that purports to regulate sexual behavior. The traditional Judeo-Christian view regards all expressions of sexuality that are not related to reproductivity as unacceptable. Even today, our country remains one of the most sexually inhibited societies in the world.[1]

The correlation of attitudes toward homosexuality and religious views or affiliations has been researched more often than any of the other factors, and none of the published studies failed to find some connection. Numerous studies, for example, found that individuals who are conservative or negative about sexuality in general and those who have more personal sex guilt are more inclined to have negative attitudes toward homosexuality.[2] More to the point, it has also been found that religious orthodoxy and traditional religious beliefs are related to negative attitudes toward homosexuality.[3] Similarly, church attendance has been correlated to conservatism and anti-homosexual attitudes.[4]

Some studies have also related homophobia to specific religions or religious denominations. Protestants and Roman Catholics, for instance, have been found to be more homophobic and more restrictive toward all sexuality than Jews, others, or people with no religious affiliation.[5] Another study found that Jews too were significantly more anti-gay than individuals with no religious affiliation.[6] Religious fundamentalists, surprisingly, were found to be only slightly more homophobic than others in two studies.[7]

Religion was also thought by many of those interviewed for this book, both parents and children, to be a stumbling block in their relationships.

(mD) The one continuing and most difficult area in my life right this moment is religion. Only recently did I realize that Christian Scientists view lesbians and gays as needing "healing." It has made me very uncomfortable. I'm not ready to leave my church, or do I see any hope of reforming it, so there remains a "grey" area.

* * * * *

(D)   Deep down in my heart I don't think
       my folks ever want to accept that
       homosexuality is okay. It just goes
       against the grain, and the Catholic
       church still says it's wrong.

                    * * * * *

(D)   My mother's turning to her religion to
       try to get away from the fact that she
       has a gay daughter.

                    * * * * *

(S)   My parents used to say, "You're going
       to hell," and I used to believe that. I
       think they probably still think that
       way.

The importance of religion to the relationships in this
book was measured in two ways. The first measurement
was based on parents' church or synagogue attendance;
either they had always attended religious services regularly
or they had not. Interestingly, though, regular attendance
did not seem to affect the relationships. Half the parents of
daughters had positive relationships and half had negative
relationships with their daughters regardless of whether or
not the parents attended religious services regularly. Parents
of sons, on the other hand, had mostly positive relationships
with their sons regardless of how often they went to
church or synagogue.

Furthermore, three-fourths of the parents in this book
were affiliated with either Roman Catholicism or a major
protestant denomination, and three-fourths of the parents
of sons were Roman Catholics. Because of the small

numbers of Jewish parents, parents affiliated with fundamentalist or other sects, and those with no religious affiliations, it was not possible for me to compare those groups to catholic and protestant parents.

That imbalance was a disappointment as my observation has been that fundamentalist parents, in particular, tend to take a rigid position with regard to their child's same-sex orientation, and parents with no religious affiliation are generally open. I have also, however, heard numerous parents from a variety of religious backgrounds identify their religious beliefs as the major obstacle in accepting their child's disclosure. Indeed, parents' religious conflicts are an important focus of at least half of the books now available for parents of lesbian daughters and gay sons.

Religious beliefs undoubtedly do present a dilemma for some parents, but, again, about half of both catholic and protestant parents of daughters in this book had positive relationships with their daughters, and the other half had negative relationships. And, once again, both sets of parents of sons had mostly positive relationships with their sons.

On closer examination, it is noted that the number of protestant parents of sons was small, only ten, and although they were one of the two most positive groups of sons' parents, the high degree of their positivity must be viewed judiciously. The fact remains, however, that both protestant and catholic parents had more positive than negative relationships with their sons.

In short, the way the parents in this book related to their lesbian daughters and gay sons, contrary to all the existing research, did not appear to be affected by whether or not they attended religious services regularly or whether they were Catholics or Prostestants. Rather, the biological sex of the child seemed to be the primary determinant of the relationships.

Education

"Tolerance of nonconformity . . . ," states sociologist Melvin Kohn, "requires a degree of analytic ability that is difficult to achieve without formal education."[8] Most studies that relate education to homophobia have supported that statement. Educated people have been found to be both more tolerant in general and more accepting of homosexuality in particular.[9] Studies of professional people, however, show that physicians, psychologists, and other mental health experts retain negative stereotypes of lesbians and gay men, and even though their attitudes might be more positive than the attitudes of less educated individuals, "a significant amount of myth and stereotyping remains despite high levels of education and training. . . ."[10]

A smaller number of studies found that education was either unrelated to homophobia or was not a strong factor in reducing prejudice.[11]

The parents in this book also presented some contradictory information on this subject. For instance, one daughter said, "My parents tend to deal with things on a very intellectual basis. They're very, very bright people. [But] I thought their attitude would be along the lines of Anita Bryant's and I was correct."

In fact, those parents of daughters with more than a high school education were something of an anomaly in that they were somewhat more likely to have *negative* relationships with their daughters than positive; education worked against the daughters in some families. This was more true of the mothers of daughters than the fathers. A recent study related to this point found that most of the college-educated mothers surveyed were open to the idea that their daughters might not marry or have children, but ninety percent of the mothers had a negative response to the idea that their daughters might have what the study called "a homosexual experience."[12]

The parents in this book, on the other hand, who had a high school education or less were about equally divided between positive and negative relationships with their lesbian daughters. In other words, daughters' parents with less education were somewhat more positive than those who had attended college, but the difference was not great.

Parents of sons were positive in both situations; fifty-nine percent of the parents with a high school education or less got along well with their sons, and ninety percent of those educated beyond high school had positive relationships. Higher levels of education just seemed to increase the degree of positivity. One son, for example, said his mother, who had not finished high school, "was never really negative. The bottom line was, 'You're my son and I love you,'" while another son described his well-educated mother as "a person very accepting of different lifestyles."

It would seem, then, that the attitudes of most parents supported the small amount of research finding education to be unrelated to homophobia. More education, in the case of some parents of daughters, even had an inverse effect. Again, parents' relationships with their daughters and sons were more determined by the sex of the child than the parents' levels of education.

Geography

Another demographic factor most researchers relate to homophobia is the place where people live or the place where they lived when they were teenagers. Studies have found that

- People raised on farms or in rural areas of the U.S. Midwest or South are highly homophobic.[13]
- People living in cities of over 250,000 population have more liberal attitudes toward homosexuality, sexual nonconformity, and androgyny in males.[14]
- People from urban areas and people who as young adolescents had lived on either the East or West Coasts are more tolerant of homosexuality.[15]

Most of the parents in this book grew up in either the Midwest or South, the most anti-gay areas of the country. This was no surprise in that nearly all the people who contributed to this book lived in the Chicago area. Parents who grew up elsewhere included those from other areas of the United States as well as several foreign countries.

Where parents grew up, nonetheless, did not seem to have much to do with the relationships. Parents of daughters from the homophobic Midwest/South remained evenly divided between positive and negative relationships with their daughters, while those parents of daughters from other areas were even somewhat more negative. Predictably, sons' parents were more positive than negative in both situations. In fact, over seventy-five percent of the sons' parents who grew up in the Midwest/South had positive relationships with their sons.

The Midwestern and Southern parents were further compared as to whether they grew up in cities of over 250,000 population or in smaller towns, farms, and rural areas. Big city parents of daughters were, once again, half negative and half positive, but almost sixty percent of those from small towns and rural areas had negative relationships with their daughters.

On the other hand, less than twenty percent of sons' parents from small towns and rural areas had negative relationships with their sons. In fact, those parents of sons from less populated areas were even more positive than parents who grew up in the supposedly more tolerant big cities, although both groups of parents of sons were more positive than negative.

Overall, it seemed that where parents grew up did not have much to do with how they related to their adult lesbian and gay children. The difference was again sex related. They were consistently positive with sons and fairly evenly divided on daughters although those daughters' parents who grew up in the rural Midwest/South were the most negative.

Parents, then, once again, contradicted the weight of the existing research and supported the small number of studies that found geography had little or no connection to homophobia.[16]

Parents' Ages

Age has also been correlated to homophobia by some researchers who found that young people are the most tolerant and that intolerance increases with age.[17] Other studies linked homophobia to a combination of age and education, church attendance, or religious affiliation.[18]

Parents of sons confirmed the age connection in that those who were fifty years of age or older at the time of the disclosure had nearly three times as many negative relationships with their sons as those who were younger than fifty when their sons came out.

Older parents of daughters, by comparison, remained evenly split between positive and negative relationships, while younger daughters' parents were more negative. One daughter contrasted her parents' ages and attitudes by saying, "My dad is seventy-nine, and he's planning for what's going to happen when my health fails . . . but my mom is almost twenty years younger, and she is looking forward to what I am going to do in the future."

In conclusion, parents of daughters neither confirmed the existing research nor supported a contradictory study that found age unrelated to homophobia.[19]

Parents' ages, in the final analysis, did not seem to be as important to the relationships as the sex of the offspring, but they did appear to have some effect, particularly on sons.

Prejudice and Politics

Parents' prejudices against people different from themselves and parents' politically conservative views resulted in a high percentage of negative relationships with both daughters and sons. Daughters were more affected than sons, but parental prejudice also produced one of the most negative groups of sons' parents. A son whose parents had had a particularly negative reaction to his disclosure recalled an earlier example of his parents' unwillingness to accept differences in people. "I wanted," he remembered, "to invite a black member of the cast from *Chorus Line* to my graduation party, and my parents told me if I did they would cancel the whole thing."

Not surprisingly, the above findings are supported by earlier research. One study, in particular, identified anti-black attitudes as the best predictor of negative attitudes toward homosexuality.[20] This finding also supported an unpublished paper which concluded that parents of a gay child who have experienced discrimination themselves as members of a minority group, were "capable of not only empathy but also true understanding" of their gay offspring.[21]

The remaining factors, those for which no published

research was found, measured the relationships according to . . .

- The length of time that had elapsed since the disclosure;
- The son's or daughter's age at the time of the disclosure;
- The number of siblings the daughter or son had; and
- The relationships that existed between parents and child as the child was growing up.[22]

Length of Time Since Disclosure

Parents of sons were, indeed, somewhat more positive when a period of five or more years followed the disclosure, although the majority of them had been positive earlier as well. One son said, "My parents probably are more totally accepting the more they see that things are going along well and that I'm a stable individual." Parents of daughters, however, became slightly *less* positive five or more years after the disclosure, and their relationships with their daughters remained rather evenly divided between positive and negative regardless of the amount of time that had elapsed.

It would seem, then, that the sex of the child was still the prime determinant here with sons having some hope of greater parental positivity after a period of time, but daughters not having the same hope.

Age at Disclosure

The sons in this book were, on the average, twenty-six years old when they came out to their parents, and the daughters were, on the average, twenty-nine years of age. Furthermore, the age of the sons when they came out appeared to have had some affect on parent-son relationships. Even though the majority of young sons' parents were positive, the percentage of positivity was higher when the sons had been at least twenty-two years old at the time of the disclosures.

The age the daughters came out had an even larger impact on the parent-daughter relationships. Those daughters who had been younger than twenty-two made up one of the most negative parent-child relationship groups. Being older, however, did not produce a high percentage of positive relationships (only fifty-four percent), but it did seem to improve the possibility of a good relationship between daughters and parents.

Thus, it appears that parents were more distressed when a young daughter or son came out, and, predictably enough, their ability to accept improved, to some extent, when the child was older, particularly if their child was a son. One son, for example, who had come out at sixteen said, "Well, they suffered it then. Now they accept it." Daughters who came out at a young age were especially vulnerable to parental disapproval. As one daughter, who was nineteen when she came out to her parents, said, "I think it would be better to wait till maybe you're twenty-five and you could say, 'I'm comfortable; I have a woman I adore, and we get along great.' "

Number of Siblings

"My folks' basic dream for me," explained one daughter whose only sibling was a brother, "was that I would marry some nice man, produce grandchildren, give them a place to visit on vacation and come home as a family unit for the holidays." Not surprisingly, those parents were extremely unhappy following their daugher's disclosure. Their reaction was not uncommon. In fact, three-fourths of the parents of only daughters and parents of daughters with just one siblling had negative relationships with their daughters, thus producing the most negative of all parent-daughter groups. By comparison, daughters with two or more siblings had many more positive parent relationships.

Paradoxically, sons with only one sibling and sons who were only children enjoyed a very high percentage of positive relationships with parents, an even higher percentage than sons with more brothers and sisters.

It was, therefore, an advantage for gay sons to come from small families, but it was a major disadvantage for lesbian daughters.

The Early Parent-Child Relationships

The unexpectedly decisive role gender played in the relationships of the family members described in this book raised a rather obvious question: Did the daughters have fewer positive relationships with their parents before they came out than the sons did? The answer in a word is yes. The fully accurate answer is more complicated. It is complicated because it is impossible to research the relationships between lesbians, gay men, and their parents without stumbling over the "cause" factor. Since 1905 when Sigmund Freud first proposed the idea that homosexuality was caused by a dominant mother and a weak father, theorists have busied themselves trying to prove or, less often, disprove his notion. "Proof" provided scholarly reputations and highly remunerative therapy practices which, in turn, shut out a graceful (or financially secure) retreat from the position that people are homosexual because their parents did something wrong. A detailed look at that subject with some new insights for parents comes later.

For now, suffice it to say that a large number of studies including the latest work from the Kinsey Institute for Sex Research identify the early relationships of parents and homosexual children as troubled, more troubled than those of parents and heterosexual children.[23] That idea, in itself, disconnected from the concept of cause and effect, hardly surprises considering the homophobic nature of our society.

The Kinsey report mentioned above, which is the careful work of Alan P. Bell, Martin S. Weinberg, and Sue Kiefer Hammersmith, made the larger point that parents' personalities and their relationships with their young children had little or no direct connection to the offspring's sexual orientation.[24] At the same time, the study also found that both lesbians and gay men had more conflict with their parents as they were growing up than heterosexuals did. Lesbian daughters, in particular, were found to have experienced more difficulty relating to both parents than heterosexual daughters, and gay sons had more trouble getting along with their fathers than nongay sons.[25]

The daughters and sons in this book were not compared to heterosexual daughters and sons. They did, however, indirectly validate the above findings in that somewhat fewer daughters than sons felt they had received a high measure of their parents' appreciation and approval while they were growing up. It would appear, then, that the child's biological sex was a factor in the relationships before the disclosures. It became an even more important factor after the disclosures.

Parents and sons who had enjoyed positive relationships as the sons were growing up were very likely to have maintained good relationships after the disclosures. In fact, the percentages of sons' positive relationships actually increased after the disclosures. Positive growing-up relationships between daughters and parents were, by comparison, at risk after the daughters came out. Only about half of them remained positive while the rest deteriorated.

In the families where the growing-up relationships were perceived by daughters and sons as negative, some of the relationships improved after the disclosures, but, predictably, most did not. The difference between daughters and sons in those instances were small, and this factor was an exception to the pattern of sons' high positivity in both sides of the factors. In fact, those parents and sons who did not get along as the sons were growing up, became the most negative of all parent-son factor groups. For daughters, negative early relationships with parents produced the third most negative factor group.

To fully answer the question, then, of the pre-disclosure balance of positive and negative relationships, it was true that there were somewhat more positive parent-son relationships to start. However, that fact alone could not explain the changed balance of positive and negative relationships that was observed after the disclosures when only sixteen percent of the sons' positive growing-up relationships compared to almost half of the daughters' became negative.

In summary, it was difficult to contrast the effects of the individual factors on daughters' relationships versus sons' relationships, because the overall pattern of differences was so consistently related to the sex of the offspring. It was nearly always a matter of how much each factor reduced or increased that central pattern.

Overall, the sons' parents were a great deal more positive than were the daughters' parents. In fact, the most positive parent-son factor was thirty percent more positive than the most positive parent-daughter factor, and, on the other end of the scale, the most negative parent-daughter factor was sixteen percent more negative than the most negative parent-son factor.

Furthermore, the pattern was one of high positivity for

sons *on both sides* of most of the factors and one of a
nearly even division of positive and negative relationships
for daughters *on both sides* of most of the factors. In other
words, the distribution of positive and negative relationships
within most of the factors was very similar to the overall
distribution of positive and negative relationships as shown
in the last chapter: The majority of sons got along well
with their parents, and only about half of the daughers had
good relationships with their parents.

The consistency of that finding made it seem clear that
the parents' primary reaction to homosexuality in their
child had depended on the biological sex of that child.
Some factors played a part in just how positive or negative
the parents were, but nothing was as important to the
parents' response as the maleness or femaleness of their
child.

Unhappy early relationships, as we have just seen, were
one exception to that rule. They resulted in a nearly equal
percentage of unhappy adult relationships for both daughters
and sons. On the other hand, coming out to parents at a
young age and parents' prejudices against people different
from themselves had negative effects on the relationships of
both daughters and sons, but the degree of negativity was
greater for daughters' relationships than sons'.

Other factors seemed to have had more impact on sons
than daughters and vice versa. Parent-son relationships, for
example, were apparently affected by the parents' levels of
education, the parents' ages at the time of the disclosures,
and the length of time since the disclosures, whereas the
number of children in the family appeared as an important
factor in the daughter-parent relationships.

And, finally, contrary to the existing research, parents'
relationships with their daughters and sons were virtually
unaffected by where the parents had grown up or by the
parents' religious affiliations and activity.

In conclusion, the risk of coming out to parents was greater for daughters than it was for sons. Sons' parents seemed to relate to sons who were also gay, while daughters' parents related to their daughters as lesbians.

* * * * *

"YES, MOTHER, A MAGAZINE SUBSCRIPTION IS A LOVELY CHRISTMAS GIFT— BUT BETTY AND I DON'T EVEN OWN A MOTORCYCLE...."

CHAPTER 6

WHY BIOLOGICAL SEX WAS SO IMPORTANT

A slightly inebriated young woman came to the bar and told
me she loved the way I had decorated the house.... "Do
you work?" she asked.... I could hardly believe my ears. I
said that I was a psychologist.

Don Clark in *Living Gay*

Until the late 1960s, homosexuality was described as
sex-role inversion. The conceptual distinction between social
sex role and sexual preference was generally not made.

Carmen de Monteflores and Stephen J. Schultz
in a paper called "Coming Out: Similarities
and Differences for Lesbians and Gay Men,"
Journal of Social Issues, 1978

When my children were growing up, I heard a riddle
that went something like this. An injured child was brought

81

to the hospital emergency room by a parent. The child's other parent was a doctor who happened to be performing surgery at the same time in the same hospital. Why, then, the riddle asked, wouldn't the child's mother give permission for the emergency room staff to treat her hurt child?

No one, including me, was able to supply the correct answer which, of course, was that the child's *mother* was the busy doctor in the operating room and therefore unavailable to sign the permission form.

It is hard to believe that biological sex defined identity quite so rigidly just twenty years ago, and yet that was the case, at least in America's heartland where I live. Biological sex at that time predetermined one set of behaviors and responsibilities for females and another, different set for males. Those differentiations are called sex roles, and they create concepts of femininity and masculinity which continue to have a major impact on how most of us look and act as well as how much education we acquire, the kind of work we do, and the overall quality of our lives. Sex roles are not innate distinctions coupled at birth to infant sex organs. They are social standards of idealized, heterosexual perceptions of women and men, and they are taught by parents and other adults to each new generation of children.

More to the point, most heterosexual women and men my age and the ages of the parents in this book had learned sex-role definitions of an ideal family that consisted of a dominant husband, a submissive wife, and obedient children. That constellation came out of primitive societies, but as recently as thirty years ago it was accepted as a standard by almost everybody. Even when, or perhaps particularly when, our birth family had differed from the ideal, as had mine, we sought as young adults to create such a family of our own. This is how we saw the individual members of such an ideal family.

The Man

The man was expected to dominate because he was physically strong. As a caveman, he had used his strength against intruders, both human and animal. In more recent times when physical strength was no longer inevitably linked to survival, man continued to demonstrate strength by competing with other males in the arenas of play, work, and, frequently, war. When he won, the man fulfilled the primary message of the male sex role: He dominated.

Silence was a necessary complement to male dominance because it concealed vulnerability. Male feelings of inadequacy, unlike those of anger which contributed to the overall appearance of strength, were stifled—errors hidden, pain denied, and tears swallowed. Expressions of affection were also limited to avoid any impression of male dependency.

The strong, silent man has also traditionally been responsible for his family. Once that meant providing a safe cave. Later it meant he was expected "to be the breadwinner and protector of his family, to do all the jobs that require physical strength, and to be the chief determiner of the couple's sex life. . . . in many families, he [was] expected to handle all the money and to make virtually every major decision."[1]

The role of father, however, beyond that of financial provider, was limited. Historically, he taught his sons the rules of survival in the wilderness. Later, he became the primary agent for handing down the prescribed sex-role differences to both his young daughters and sons, and he maintained a particularly keen interest in seeing that his sons adhered to the standards of the male sex role.[2] The traditional father's responsibility, on the other hand, never included the day-to-day care of his children.

Indeed, fatherhood has never been, nor is it today, the

strong suit of the ideal male. Men might well be called Silent Fathers. A Silent Father is not uniquely the father of a lesbian daughter or gay son; he is nearly everybody's father, a man restricted by obsolete sex-role definitions.

Men tend to camouflage their tender feelings toward children, to express them in rough-housing: a mock punch instead of a hug; telling a six-year-old boy on his way to a birthday party to "give 'em hell" when that isn't what is meant at all.[3]

* * * * *

The "masculine mystique" has discouraged males from learning to relate to people, including children, in a compassionate, warm, open, affectionate manner. The instrumental orientation they have been taught all their lives leads them to praise their children's successes but ill equips them to sympathize with their bumbling errors. They are thus able to offer "conditional affection" only.[4]

* * * * *

. . . fathers were apt to say that they tried to solve marital (and parental) problems either by saying nothing and hoping problems would work out or by leaving the house.[5]

* * * * *

The average man is more "phantom man" than "family man." As a father he is largely absent. Even when he is present he is absent—there in body, but in every other respect removed from the family. Present or absent, the father is relying on his spouse to relate to the children for him.[6]

The Silent Father's spouse was usually prepared to relate to the children for him. She operated under a very different set of sex-role tenets.

The Woman

The ancient woman was expected to be submissive because she was considered physically weaker than the man. As the caveman's helpmate and in return for his protection, she cooked his meals over an open fire and bore and tended his children.

Later when I and the other mothers in this book were young, the ideal woman was still expected to be submissive. We fulfilled the primary message of the ancient female sex role by marrying, having children, and spending the rest of our lives caring for our families. Indeed, we are the literal mothers of what is now called the baby boom generation.

The woman's primary responsibility, according to the traditional sex role, was to nurture, supply nourishment. She suckled. She also planned what her children and husband would eat, shopped for it, cooked it, and cleaned up after it had been eaten. In addition, nurturing included the daily care and training of young children.

The woman, again unlike the man, was, by sex-role definition, dependent, and she was allowed to witness her dependence by displaying certain emotions. She could, for example, under some conditions, cry; she could also express feelings of inadequacy such as fear. In addition, she was encouraged to display affection, to be openly warm and loving. In short, the feelings of women that identified them in the eyes of men as submissive and dependent were acceptable under sex-role rules, while other emotions that suggested strength, such as anger, were not.

To summarize, the female strengthened and enhanced the male through default. His dominance defined her submission.

In truth, both women and men lost to the sex-role hierarchy. She was forced into subservient dependence, and he was overloaded with responsibility and robbed of intimacy.

Their children lost too. And we shall see that if their children grew up to love others of the same sex, they lost twice. Lesbian daughters lost three times.

The Children

Once when Jason was still too young to walk, I playfully dressed him in one of his older sister's dresses and put him on the front lawn in his jump chair to await his father. His father's outraged response on being greeted by a male infant in a dress was such that I not only never did such a thing again, but I remember the incident twenty-five years later.

My story illustrates the importance parents, particularly fathers, attach to distinguishing a male infant's gender. And, indeed, parents' differentiation of boys and girls is a fundamental emphasis during the early years of child-raising. The result is called "sex typing," an expressed preference by childen for toys and activities that adults consider appropriate to their sex, something which is accomplished in the average child by the age of four.[7]

By definition, most parents of my generation wanted

their sons to be "real boys" and their daughters to be "little ladies," and this is what we had in mind.

> In the United States a *real* boy climbs trees, disdains girls, dirties his knees, plays with soldiers, and takes blue for his favorite color. When they go to school, real boys prefer manual training, gym, and arithmetic. In college the boys smoke pipes, drink beer, and major in engineering or physics.[8]

A daughter was a "little lady" if she colored inside the lines, admired boys, sat so as not to show her underpants, played with dolls, and took pink for her favorite color. When they went to school, little ladies preferred reading and home economics. In college, traditional girls minored in teaching and nursing and majored in finding a husband.

Certainly the primary messages of the two sex roles were evident in these brief descriptions of the idealized children of a not too distant time. The boy grew up to be dominant because he was aggressive and well educated, and the girl grew up to be submissive because she was well prepared to marry and have children.

"Parents," wrote feminist Letty Cottin Pogrebin, "have built a prison of gender, brick by brick."[9] The analogy of a sex-role prison is far from inaccurate. The chief message of the sex roles to children was, after all, obedience.

Why Sex Roles Matter to Us

Sex roles have a potent meaning to lesbians, gay men, and their parents. In the first place, numerous studies show that a belief in rigid sex-role stereotyping correlates to homophobia. One study even identified the best single predictor of homophobia as "a belief in the traditional family ideology, i.e., dominant father, submissive mother, and obedient children" and the second best predictor as "agreement with traditional beliefs about women, e.g., that it is worse for a woman to tell dirty jokes than it is for a man."[10] Importantly, all of the researchers who studied this point found a connection between traditional sex roles and homophobia.

Furthermore, the early assimilation of sex-role ideals grants them a validity that few adults ever challenge. Sociologist Joseph Harry confirms this point.

> People, particularly males, rarely question the ideal nature of gender ideals. Rather, they more commonly question the adequacy with which they or others approximate those ideals. Many seem indignantly proud of their loyalty to those ideals and question the gender-adequacy of persons who question gender ideals. . . . An effect of this is that gender ideals are infrequently reflected upon and intelligence becomes virtually inoperative in the area of gender.[11]

In the second place, sex roles themselves generate homophobia. They are, of course, primarily sexist, but their inherent sexism is antecedent to homophobia. "The male role," said author Gregory Lehne, "is predominantly maintained by men themselves. Men devalue homosexuality, then use this norm of homophobia to control other men in their males roles."[12] Any male who has been goaded with the taunt "faggot" understands full well that the implicit message of the male sex role is homophobic. In fact, homophobia empowers machismo.

The third importance of sex roles comes from the idea,

identified in the quotations at the beginning of this chapter, that lesbians and gay men pose a threat to traditional sex roles. The challenge they seem to present may be apparent as they are growing up, or it may not be recognized until after they come out, but it is almost inevitably perceived to exist by parents sooner or later. That is not to say that parents always, or even frequently, understand their daughter or son as a challenge in a cognitive way. More often, I think, parents feel an undefined dis-ease with regard to their child, feelings not clearly understood or verbalized, but strong feelings nonetheless.

The response of parents to such a perceived challenge varies according to the strength of the individual parent's belief system and also according to whether the parent is a mother or a father. The response further varies according to who presents the challenge, a daughter or a son.

In simple terms, I believe it is the dichotomy of traditional sex roles that creates many of the problems in our families. Parents who hold rigid sex-role definitions of acceptable and unacceptable behavior not only limit their own enjoyment of their children, but restrict the freedom of those daughters and sons, both as they are growing up and after they become adults, to know and like themselves as they are.

Sex roles, probably more than anything else, are the unrecognized, stubborn dandelion root of conflict between lesbians, gay men, and their parents.

* * * * *

"Morris, you can take credit for his homosexuality, but I've got dibs on his chutzpah."

CHAPTER 7

SEX ROLES: PARENTS AND SONS

I think when I was young the thing that estranged me from my brothers and sisters and from my father especially was the fact that I listened to classical music. That used to drive them crazy.

A Son

... the most frightening feature of childhood for many gays was the distance between them and their fathers, and the feeling that resolution of the conflict was, and is, hopeless.

Dr. Charles Silverstein
in *Man to Man, Gay Couples in America*

Fathers of Sons

Sixty-five percent of the fathers and sons in this book shared positive relationships after the sons came out. What is more, the same-sex parents of sons were the second most positive parents after mothers of sons; they were more positive than either mothers or fathers of adult daughters.

These facts surprise. They challenge the life experience of many gay sons. They challenge the notion that fathers are "threatened" by gay sons. They challenge the stereotype of the Hostile-Detached father of a gay son.

Several things might explain the relatively high positivity of the fathers.

- The actual number of fathers of sons is considerably smaller than the number of mothers. Divorce, death, and estrangement account for this fact. It is possible that the more negative fathers are simply no longer a part of their sons' lives.
- The Chicago-area sons in this book may be substantially different from the sons living in, say, San Francisco, in that the majority of them have remained physically close to their families, and, as a result, they and their fathers now interact as two male adults.
- The cause-related literature that identifies fathers of gay sons as hostile and detached all depicts the growing-up relationships of sons with fathers, not adult sons and fathers, and more than a few relationships between fathers and sons improved after the sons came out.

It was also true that early conflict between fathers and sons was no stranger to the families in this book. Such conflict was part of just under half the father-son relationships. In particular, those boys who had transgressed their fathers' teachings with regard to sex-role distinctions described push-me-pull-me relationships with their fathers. Parents', especially fathers', fear of effeminacy puts boys, according to Letty Cottin Pogrebin, "under severe sex role pressure to achieve something called 'manhood'—which boys must earn and re-earn by establishing the many ways they are different from women."[1] The intensity of the father-son conflict varied in accordance with both the extent of the father's insistence on sex-role conformity and the extent of the son's nonconformity.

One of the most negative relationships, for instance, was that of a son who described his father as "the American male, the role model of 'I'm the breadwinner. I'm the dominant one in the family. I'm going to run this family the way I think it should be run.'" The son also said

> My father used to beat me very severely . . . fists, and one time he took a ball bat to me. He wanted me to grow up like him and really get into his macho stuff, but my tendencies really weren't to that.

More commonly, however, a nonviolent sense of difference separated sons and their same-sex parents. Father-son dissimilarity was also noted by Bell and his associates who found that almost three-fourths of their gay male respondents had felt "very little" or "not at all" like their fathers as they were growing up.[2] One of the fathers in this book provided an example of such father-son distance.

> I tried to bring the things into my son's life that I like. I love the ocean. I love ships. I tried to bring nautical things like a big anchor I made once to go on the wall of his room. I'd try to go swimming with him. He just went along with it, but he never really liked it. It turned out that he loved movies

and records. Movies and records I can take
or leave. I don't think I ever bought a
record in my life.*

In conclusion, just under half the sons in this book
remembered their fathers as either having withheld appreciation and approval when they were between the ages
of seven and twenty-one or as having given them unevenly
so that the sons were never sure what to expect from their
fathers. Furthermore, nearly all the sons who felt their
fathers had consistently appreciated and approved of them
as they were growing up, described Silent Fathers who were
"always real busy," were not "really affectionate," were
"less affectionate than my mother," "did not express emotions well," and "did not communicate as well as anyone
else in my family." One son described his father this way

My father certainly was pretty distant and
removed. He was very friendly, and I knew
that he loved us. I knew that he loved my
mother and that he was very hard working,
but he never exactly knew our names. He
would say, "George . . . Robbie . . . Mark
. . . bring me that wrench." So I never felt
he really knew me, and I would say my
father was, in general, rather distant.

---

*Both of the father-son relationships described above are now
defined as positive. The first son has maintained close contact with
his family, including his father, and while the father does not openly
acknowledge his son's same-sex orientation, he has for many years
welcomed his son, his son's lover, and other gay friends to the family
home.

Equally important, father-son conflicts and Silent Fathers called up certain responses from the wives and mothers in these families.

Mothers of Sons

Mothers of sons were the most positive parents; seventy-six percent of the mother-son relationships were positive. These facts do not surprise. Loving relationships between gay men and their mothers are almost legendary. They have been as devalued by the unkind eye of research as they have been valued and enjoyed by the mothers and sons themselves.

When these relationships are viewed from a sex-role perspective rather than from a "cause" bias, they take on a new dimension. As the opposite-sex parent, as the primary caretaker of children, as the communicator between fathers and children, as the openly affectionate parent, and as the thermostatic regulator of the family's emotional climate, the mother reacts out of her own distinctly different sex-role socialization by attempting to put an end to the father-son tug of war. Her greatest empathy, nevertheless, is often with the boy who, first of all, is a child to be protected, and, second, like the mother herself, is being penalized for differentiating from the male idealization. As a result, an advocate relationship develops between mother and son. As one son put it, "Whatever tendencies of being gay I had, I think my mother more readily accepted than my father did."

In our family, for example, I supported Jason's industry and ingenuity the summer he was thirteen and developed an enthusiastic market in the neighborhood for his home-made bread. His father, on the other hand, did not feel enthusiasm for his young son's project. The three of us argued that summer over all manner of things related to bread baking—an overheated kitchen, orders phoned in at dinnertime, and so forth. We never, as I remember, addressed Herman's real concern: that the "masculinity" of an adolescent boy who chooses to spend his summer vacation in a kitchen is suspect. The shadow-boxing dynamic that was established that summer became a familiar pattern of disagreement in our family until Jay came out to us six years later. It was not a happy time in our lives. In fact, Jason survived adolescence by spending as much time as possible behind his bedroom door attached to stereo headphones.

Psychologist Don Clark made the point that, "Gay youngsters grow up in a lonely, unfriendly world." He went on to say . . .

> It is during these years that Gay youngsters often build an invisible wall between themselves and their parents. It is built as a protection. They have listened carefully and seen no sign that their parents are likely to be supportive if their Gay identity is discovered. The more open and sharing they are with parents, the more likely is the discovery. Hence, the transparent wall is erected and parents wonder why their offspring has suddenly become so uncommunicative.[3]

There was such a wall in our family. It served as a shield for Jason who, as an adolescent with a strong if not clearly defined sense of self, resisted the inappropriateness of his parents' heterosexual message. His father and I, on the other hand, offered no alternatives.

In short, a common pattern of interaction occurred between parents and gay sons as the sons were growing up. That pattern was tempered by the personalities and backgrounds of the individuals involved, but its fundamental order was derived from traditional sex roles. The Silent Father was intent on propelling his son into "real boy" and "man's man" models. The son was bewildered and sometimes angered by a sense of difference from his father, and no matter how close or how far he was from his father's male ideals, that feeling of difference persisted. One son said, "My dad's idea of love was trying to wrestle with me. That is not the way I would express love, and I would just get mad. It was hard for us to communicate." The nurturing mother responded to the father-son conflict by "rescuing" the son. "My mother and I were very close," another son said, "but there was a stress relationship with my father, and although my family seemed to think he was very affectionate toward me, I never felt that."

Fathers and Mothers of Gay Sons

As the son grew up and then came out to his parents, the family dynamic changed. The mother-son closeness was in place, and if the son valued that closeness, the good relationship between mother and son was likely to continue. The father-son conflict, on the other hand, lessened after the adult son came out. It lessened because the Silent Father had a lifetime of sex-role induced experience that allowed him to withdraw from the situation, and that is precisely what nearly all the fathers did. Some did it faster and with more finality than others.

One father, for example, who learned within a week that both of his sons were gay, refused to talk about it according to his wife. "He viewed it," she remembered, "as if to say, 'Their arms are broken. Get a doctor, and I'll pay the bill. Don't concern me with it.' "

Another father told his son, "Lead your life somewhere, but don't be around me." A son simply said, "My father and I very rarely talk about it."

As Marc Feigen Fasteau said in his book, *The Male Machine,* "It is hard for a man to begin the process of getting to know his children at the age of forty-five. He doesn't really know what they're like and, more important, he doesn't know how to talk to them."[4] Undoubtedly the heterosexual father of a homosexual son is even more inhibited; in a significant sense, he literally does not know what his son is like. One son, for instance, said his father had "never expressed unhappiness about [my gayness], although I know that he is probably unhappy about it. It's been like, 'Well, if that's the way it is, then that's the way it is.' "

In most sons' families, two things happened next which I believe explain teh high positivity of parents of sons. First, gay sons were likely to remain gay sons. The sons in this book came out to their parents at a younger age than did the daughters, and very few of them later engaged in heterosexual contact.[5] Consequently, as time passed, the parents of sons had good reason to understand that their sons were indeed gay and not just going through a phase of sexual experimentation. This in itself did not lead to positive parents, but it gave a constancy to the parent-son relationships; it allowed parents to resign themselves.

Second, the majority of sons eventually accomplished something that *did* lead to positive relationships with parents: They fulfilled the primary message of the male sex role! That message, as we remember, is a measure of dominance defined through competition. Sons, both gay and nongay, compete with other men and, in a fundamental way, with their own fathers. Despite the relative youth of the sons in this book, who were, on the average, twenty-six years old, and despite the fact that forty percent of them were still in school, just over half the sons already had either more education or more prestigious jobs than their fathers. Some fathers, of course, may have been challenged by their sons' accomplishments, but, in a larger sense, the sons were more likely to be a source of pride to their parents. This idea is supported by two of the factors presented in Chapter 5. Although the majority of all the parents of sons were positive in both situations, they were even more positive if their son was twenty-two years old or older when he came out and if five or more years had passed since the disclosure. Both factors allowed the necessary time for sons to mature and evidence financial independence.

One situation contradicted this pattern. Those sons whose employment included repeated media identification of them as openly gay men were less likely to earn their parents' approval through their work. One such son, whose family had objected for years to such media attention, pointed out the contradiction when he said, "If you substituted the word 'Joliet' for 'gay community,' my mother would be very proud of me. 'Oh, yes,' she could say, 'he writes for the Joliet newspaper or he serves on the board of directors of the Joliet hospital.' "

Indeed, this is not to say that a simplistic correlation exists between sons' educational or career achievements and parental positivity. In fact, with few exceptions, the sons who had negative relationships with their parents were also successful competitors. In those families, however, other factors seemed to have taken precedence. Two sons, for example, had older gay siblings whose relationships with the parents in those families were also troubled. Another son's father, who no longer lived with the family, was both the product of a machismo culture and a gay man himself.

Three other sons demonstrated the negative impact of factors identified earlier in that one's mother was in her late seventies at the time of the disclosure, and two had had exceedingly poor growing-up relationships with their parents. The few remaining negative parent-son relationships were enigmas; no reason or reasons presented an explanation of their negativity.

Then, too, a number of sons whose relationships were positive had, to some degree, disappointed parents who saw them as providers of grandchildren. Even though fatherhood is an undervalued component of the male ideal, one son said, "My mother's greatest concern is grandchildren; her dream was a grandchild." Another son described a mother's disappointment that emanated from what she called "a death of one branch of the family." Even within positive relationships, sons with no brothers, only-children sons, and some ethnic sons may have amplified parents' regret over the probable loss of grandchildren.

In the final analysis, all the parents and sons were restricted and damaged by the homophobic, sexist content of sex roles. Parents were at odds, and fathers and young sons, in particular, lost the opportunity to understand and know one another. The majority of parents and sons, however, did manage to achieve positive relationships later. In contrast, daughters and their parents told a strikingly different story.

* * * * *

Untitled Work by artist, Kara Barnard. All Rights Reserved, The Naiad Press, Inc.

CHAPTER 8

SEX ROLES: PARENTS AND DAUGHTERS

Much of our identity is rooted in the family's expectations of us [and] in one crucial way gay people do not fit family expectations.

Betty Berzon, Ph.D.
in *Positively Gay*

Relationships based on fixed forms where dependency was a central feature may no longer be comfortable or tolerable.

John M. Schneider, M.D.
in *Stress, Loss and Grief*

Mothers of Daughters

Sex roles remained a key factor in the daughters' interactions with their parents. Their relationships differed most dramatically from the parent-son relationships after the daughters came out. Why that was true is probably related to the fact that both the daughters and mothers in this book were part of the first generation of women to challenge the restrictions of the traditional female sex role.

Whether or not the mothers and daughters were active participants in the women's movement, they all lived through and were affected by enormous social change as a result of that movement. In particular, a daughter who was born between 1955 and 1970, as almost half of the daughters in this book were, was exposed to changing expectations for girls and women. She was likely to have been socialized by parents according to traditional sex roles and then given different, even conflicting, messages by parents and others as she grew up and became an adult. The mother's role during those years was equally confused. By virtue of the fact that she herself was a mother, she had met the primary message of the traditional female sex role, but she had also become increasingly aware that her young daughter's life had more options than had been available to her when she was young.

Many mothers of that time ignored the confusion, and, like the mothers of older daughters, raised their girls to marry and have children, leaving the underlying message of submission intact. Other mothers incorporated new messages of equality into the traditional role and thereby passed along a contradictory direction that said, "Be like me, but don't be like me." In other words, mothers encouraged their daughters to educate themselves so they could have careers and compete equally with males in the marketplace, the underlying message, of course, being dominance; but, at the same time neither mothers nor fathers waivered from the traditional message to daughters: marry and have babies, in that order. If the contradiction was accounted for, and often it was not, the solution given to daughters was to build careers first and have babies later.

Those, then, were the two forms of sex-role message given by the parents in this book to their daughters. The newer message contained some ambiguity, but it did, nonetheless, retain the traditional script of heterosexual marriage and children. To that extent, both messages to daughters held an element of submission.

In the early years as the daughters were growing up, they experienced an almost identical pattern of conflict with their mothers, the daughters' same-sex parents, as the young sons had experienced with their same-sex parents, the fathers. Approximately half of the daughters remembered having pleased their mothers, and fifty-two percent of the daughters thought their mothers had either withheld appreciation and approval or had given it unevenly as they were growing up.

One daugher, for example, remembered, "I always felt inferior and not wanted because my mother truthfully said she preferred my sister over me." Another daughter said her mother would be "affectionate one minute, then all of a sudden she was real angry and cold. It got to the point where I didn't trust it anymore."

The early mother-daughter conflict, on the other hand, was overall less violent than that between the young sons and their fathers; it was less a tug-of-war and more something that might be called a tug-of-love. It was also true, according to the Bell, Weinberg, Hammersmith study that daughters' feelings of dissimilarity to their mothers were less common than they had been between sons and fathers. Only forty-five percent of their lesbian respondents had felt different from their mothers as they were growing up.[1] Several factors explain why the early relationships of mothers and daughters were less discordant than those between fathers and sons.

- Mothers, as women, are less prone to violent behavior than fathers, as men.
- Mothers, as primary caretakers of children, are thought to be more affectionate and less competitive with both daughters and sons than are fathers.[2]
- Homophobia, as less intrinsic to both the traditional and the new female sex role than it is to the male sex role, allows girls more latitude than boys with regard to sex-role teaching. Some mothers as well as some fathers even reward and encourage a young daughter's participation in activities traditionally assigned to sons, and the changing female sex role strengthened that inclination on the part of parents.

Nevertheless, early conflict did exist between daughters and mothers in about half the families, and that fact may have been instrumental in bringing about a response from fathers that was similar to the response of mothers of young sons.

Fathers of Daughters

Sixty-five percent of the fathers had positive relationships with their daughters as the daughters were growing up. That statistic challenges the cause-biased caricature of a hostile, detached, wife-dominated male which has been unilaterally applied to fathers of both gay sons and lesbian daughters. It also, however, presents a challenge to our own characterization of the Silent Father, and Silent Fathers of daughters were as evident in the interviews as Silent Fathers of sons. One daughter, for instance, said, "I've only recently gotten to know my father. What I remember was that he was never home, and when he wasn't working, he was sleeping." Another daughter also remembered a father who traveled during the week. "Then," she said, "he'd come home on the weekends, he'd be very tired, and you'd kind of tiptoe around." Importantly, though, she added, "There was always a warmness and a closeness."

Many of the fathers, then, were unexpectedly positive influences in their young daughters' lives. Paternalism in its most agreeable form is, after all, a familiar characteristic of father-daughter relationships. As opposite-sex parents, these fathers somehow overcame work-related absences and the male sex-role inhibition against intimacy, in at least sixty-five percent of the families, in order to let their young daughters know they were appreciated and approved of by their fathers if not their mothers. They, too, like the mothers of young sons who were in conflict with their fathers, may have been protecting and "rescuing" their daughters from the mothers' displeasure.

Thus, the picture of young daughters and parents is very like the picture of young sons and parents: About half of both daughters and sons remembered their same-sex parents as having withheld appreciation and approval, and a majority of both daughters and sons remembered having received a high measure of appreciation and approval from their opposite-sex parents. The primary difference was the degree of support offered by the opposite-sex parents; mothers of sons were somewhat more positive than fathers of daughters, and that difference is probably best understood as resulting from the behavior and responsibility distinctions of the two sex roles.

In contrast, however, a sharp difference appeared after the daughters came out. Unlike the majority of parent-son relationships which either remained positive or evolved positively after the sons came out, daughters had fewer positive relationships after they came out, and, in particular, their fathers were less positive than they had been earlier.

Mothers and Fathers of Lesbian Daughters

Mothers and fathers responded to their daughters' disclosures out of their own sex-role expectations. Virtually all of the daughters had been socialized to grow up, get married, and have children, and when those daughters grew up to love women instead of men, they failed to comply with the submissive message of the traditional female sex role. They also lost the economic and status advantages available to women who marry men and thereby caused their parents concern. Finally, as self-supporting women, they posed a threat to the male hierarchy by actively competing in the workplace. Parents of daughters, then, were both concerned and fearful as were the parents of sons, but they were also uniquely uncomfortable with their daughters' places in the world.

Furthermore, the negative feelings of daughters' parents were less inclined to moderate over time for two reasons. First, the daughters did not have the same potential as the sons had for eventual fulfillment of the primary sex-role requirement. They were far less likely to marry men someday than were the sons likely to succeed in their careers.

The second reason is solidly linked to the first. The daughters in this book, far more than the sons, had given their parents reason to think they were going through a phase of sexual experimentation. The evidence was a much higher pre-disclosure incidence among the daughters of heterosexual dating, engagements, marriages, and existing children. In addition, many more daughters than sons facilitated their parents' hope for a heterosexual marriage in the future. One daughter explained it this way.

> I chose to tell my mother that, "Yeah, maybe someday down the line I'll get married." That's not really a lie. I don't know. I don't hate men. So I really wasn't telling my mother a lie, although I most likely will not marry a man. I also knew she really didn't want to hear that. I caused her a lot less trauma than if I had come out and curtly said, "No, I'm never going to get married."

Another daughter included an explanation of political choice in her disclosure, information she recognized caused her mother to continue hoping for a change three and a half years after the disclosure.

> I related to things like compulsory heterosexuality, that I in fact did have choices and that there wasn't only one choice in the world, only one way. There was *my* choice and my way. It was difficult to explain those things. I'm sure they were words my parents had never heard before. My mother still relates to the fact that I *chose* it, because she thinks if I chose it, I can *un*choose it and do something else.

A third daughter said

> I dated a dozen or so boys, and I had one girlfriend that was very special to me at fifteen, sixteen, seventeen, but when I told

> my mom at nineteen, she was not thrown
> but *surprised.* She still wishes I was maybe
> bi; maybe she'd settle for bi. See, I confuse
> my parents. . . .

Mothers, in particular, seemed confused by their lesbian daughters. Exactly half of their relationships were positive and half were negative. Such a statistical split, similar to the early mother-daughter division of relationships, suggests a complex reaction on the part of mothers. One daughter illustrated that possibility when she said, "For years my mother told me, 'Don't get pregnant,' but after she knew I was gay, she told me she'd rather see me pregnant or dead." Another daughter said, "My mother had always stuck up for me. She had been my backer, and I felt she thought this was a slap in the face."

A third daughter, who said her mother refused to recognize her capacity to love a woman, identified one possible explanation for such a refusal.

> My mother says confusing things to me that
> don't make logical sense. For instance, she
> tells me it's just *lust,* not love. I don't think
> my mother easily accepts the idea of me
> loving someone else besides her, especially
> another woman. I think that's very threaten-
> ing to her. It's like mothers who are
> threatened by their sons' wives, but somehow
> it becomes more strained, an extreme case
> of it, when the daughter is a lesbian.

Another daughter, who was formerly married, contrasted her mother's past behavior toward her husband to her mother's present behavior toward her lover.

> My mother used to flirt with my husband,
> fix him special foods, and things like that,
> but she can't compete for attention now.
> She is unable to flatter my lover who is a
> very successful business person with an MBA
> from a prestigious school. My lover is polite
> to my mother, and all that, but she's not
> flattered by her.

The idea that mothers may feel displaced by the significant women in their daughters' lives is strengthened by research which shows that mothers who are primarily homemakers, as were the two mothers above, tend to replace their own sense of identity with a reflected definition of themselves that is based on their children's identities.[3] Some mothers, then, as same-sex parents of lesbian daughters, probably experienced a greater sense of displacement than did the fathers of sons, who saw themselves as men first and fathers second.

In addition, a surprising number of daughters perceived their mothers to be "latent" or "closet" lesbians. Those perceptions are included here because they were not solicited by interview questions but were spontaneously offered, and virtually no comparable information was offered by sons with regard to their fathers.

> My mother didn't like my ex-girlfriend. I
> don't know if it was that particular person,
> or if it was some kind of jealousy. I think
> gay women make her nervous; she just doesn't
> know how to react to them. I think that's
> because she was a latent homosexual herself.

* * * * *

My mother's reaction to me being a lesbian never made much sense to me. I thought, well, maybe she's a lesbian and just never came out.

* * * * *

My father's so kind of laissez faire about everything, but my mother had a little bit of trouble with me as a lesbian. She'd *kill* me if she ever thought I said it, but if my mother were my age now, I think she'd be a lesbian.

* * * * *

One night my mother asked my lover and me to play bingo with her. A friend of hers was coming. Well, my lover and I went to the church, and I just about dropped my teeth. The woman was more than very tailored; she looked as though she would be in place at any woman's bar. She and my mother were just joking and laughing, but once you're out you *always* know. I got a kick out of it, really, and my lover said, "I don't believe this."

* * * * *

My mother marched into the bookstore and said, "I've decided to be a political lesbian. I'm coming out." I thought the woman who owned the bookstore was going to fall on the floor.

There was, of course, no way to assess the accuracy of the above perceptions which may have been less the product of some mothers' actual unexpressed lesbianism than the result of some mothers' unexpressed envy of their daughters' independence. Either eventuality, however, held the potential to further complicate the relationships of mothers and daughters.

The changing sex role for women, as we have already noted, provided yet another explanation of mothers' response to daughters. The daughters in this book had, on the average, three and a half years of education beyond high school, and nearly all were career women with good jobs. The mothers, therefore, may have been juggling pride in their daughters' accomplishments with a combined sense of concern for them as unmarried women and an aversion to their lesbianism. In particular, those mothers who held traditional views of women had reason to be confused. Research has shown that women who oppose feminist goals tend to avoid risks, resist change, and have lower levels of curiosity and flexibility.[4]

Those characteristics described some of the mothers of both daughters and sons, and the chances are good that they created an extra barrier for the mothers of daughters. One daughter, for example, who held two degrees and was in the process of establishing her own professional business, described her mother as "very much oriented toward home and family, raising her kids and keeping her house." She went on to say, "My mother can't relate at all to what I'm doing."

Two mothers who had been active feminists before their daughters came out supported the idea in that they were also some of the most positive mothers of daughters.

When I joined the National Organization for

Women in 1974, I became educated as to the discrimination facing lesbians and gays. It was one of the many issues I worked on, and legislation I lobbied on. I have, since joining NOW, had very good friends who are lesbians, and who have spent a lot of time in our home.

* * * * *

The people and events in my daughter's life are basically the same as what's going on in my life. I mean, she's into nuclear arms protest and a lot of social issues that I'm interested in, so we kind of compare notes. They have a strong group that is lobbying for a stop to the nuclear arms race. They're putting themselves on the line. I visit the women's coffee house with my daughter and listen to their speakers and so forth. It's been a good experience for me; I've learned a lot.

The first mother was uniquely prepared to hear a daughter's disclosure. The second mother had discovered a strong bond with her lesbian daughter who was also a feminist.

Several factors, then, were seen as contributing to the evenly divided pattern of mothers' relationships with daughters: The reflected identities of some mothers that caused them to feel displaced; the resistance of some mothers to a changing sex role for women; and the possibility that some mothers envied their daughters' lives. In addition, the past heterosexual experiences of many daughters, as well as the ongoing facilitation of others, resulted in a continuing hope on the part of many mothers and fathers that their daughters would eventually marry a man and have a family. All four factors are related to sex roles.

Moreover, the changing sex role for women undoubtedly had a stronger impact on the daughters' relationships than the sons'. To daughters and mothers it offered the potential for both greater distance and increased closeness. Its impact on fathers of lesbian daughters, however, was more consistently negative. Even the one father who had "always prided himself on being a feminist," had an exceedingly negative reaction to his daughter's disclosure.

In fact, fifty-eight percent of the adult daughter-father relationships were negative. That figure is twenty-three percent more negative than it was as the daughters were growing up, and it accounted for all of the deterioration of daughter-parent relationships. It also described the most negative group of parent-child relationships. Unlike the fathers of sons who became more positive after their sons came out; unlike the opposite-sex mothers of sons who maintained their positivity; and, finally, unlike the mothers of daughters who remained equally divided, over half of the positive father-daughter relationships became negative after the disclosures.

Fathers were clearly troubled by lesbian daughters. In one way they were very like the fathers of sons: They withdrew. Nearly all of them had been Silent Fathers before their daughters came out, and they became even more silent afterward. One daughter said, "When my father and I are alone in the room, it's very uncomfortable. We don't have a lot to say to each other." Another daughter described a very limited communication with her father.

> Now when I call over there, he'll answer the phone. He'll say, "Hello, how are you?" and I'll say, "Fine." Then he'll say, "You want to talk to your mother, right?" and I say,

"Yeah." That's it. The conversation is always
the same.

A third daughter said, "My father has *never* said anything
to me about [being a lesbian]. He tightens his lips and just
goes off in his world in this stare."

Silent Fathers of adult daughters, however, managed to
communicate their disapproval. One daughter said, "He can
look me right in the eye and say, 'I love you,' and I can
see the hate around it. I don't think it's a false perception
on my part. You can't fool somebody you'd known for
twenty years." It was also not difficult to connect fathers'
disapproval to sex roles. Eighty percent of these daughters
were either the first or the only daughter in their families,
factors which would have heightened both parents' expectations for the daughter's eventual marriage and motherhood.
In addition, over seventy percent of the daughters who had
negative relationships were better educated than their fathers,
thereby producing the possibility of outstripping the fathers'
career accomplishments. Indeed, quite a number of daughters
already had more prestigious, if not better paying, jobs
than their fathers.

While similar accomplishments by sons had served as a
source of pride to their parents, daughters' educational and
career achievements probably had the opposite effect on
fathers who were intolerant of women's nontraditional role
behavior. As one relevant study observed, "Both gay and
feminist movements do suggest a blurring and annihilation
of the distinctions between the sexes and stir the same
deep emotions in opposition."[5] This point is supported
further by the factor in Chapter 5 that showed no improve-
ment in the parent-daughter relationships over time. Sons'
parents did become more positive five years or more after
the disclosures, but daughters' parents did not.

In fact, even the two most liberal fathers had difficulty accepting their lesbian daughters.

> I was a typical girl, but my father always wanted to make sure I knew other things too and that I'd be able to take care of myself. He used to drill into me, "They're going to tell you you can't do this and you can't do that because you're a female, and you're a black female, but don't believe it! You can do anything you want." [But] he really didn't want me to be *that* independent, because once I was, he and I just had a terrible time.

The second daughter had a similar experience with both her father and mother after she came out.

> They undercut everything they had always told me they valued about me which was my independence, my ability to think for myself and to make my own decisions. Basically, what they did was snatch all that back and say, "You've gone too far."

Those daughters, on the other hand, who described positive father relationships were not less accomplished than the daughters with negative fathers. In fact, they were equally as well educated in comparison to their fathers as the other daughters. They were also, on the average, approximately the same age. They were, however, significantly different in two ways: Over eighty percent had had positive growing-up relationships with their fathers, and, importantly, ninety-one percent had at least one heterosexual sister. It was also true that the daughters with positive fathers had, on the average, more siblings than the daughters with negative fathers.

In short, a father was more inclined to relate positively to a lesbian daughter if he had appreciated and approved of her as a girl and if he had several other children including at least one daughter who could be expected to marry and have children. And, to sharpen the point, a lesbian daughter younger than twenty-two who was either the first or the only daughter in a small family and who also exceeded her father's educational or career achievements probably presented a double anathema to her father even when they had gotten along well as she was growing up.

Again, sexism and homophobia generated by sex roles had impinged upon all the daughter-parent relationships at one time or another as they had on all the son-parent relationships. The results, however, were more confusing and more negative for daughters and their families. Lesbian daughters had, in the final analysis, lost three times: as women, as young daughters of mothers, and as adult daughters of both parents. Their parents had also lost the opportunity to know their daughters.

* * * * *

"Distant father, close-binding mother."

From: *Relax! This Book Is Only A Phase You Are Going Through*, by Charles Ortleb and Richard Fiala. St. Martin's Press, Inc., New York, Copyright © 1978 by Charles Ortleb and Richard Fiala. Reprinted with permission.

CHAPTER 9*

WHY PARENTS ASK "WHAT DID WE DO WRONG?"

I know what you must be thinking now. You're asking
yourself: What did we do wrong? How did we let this
happen? Which one of us made him that way?

I can't answer that, Mama. In the long run, I guess I
really don't care. All I know is this: If you and Papa are
responsible for the way I am, then, I thank you with all my
heart, for it's the light and joy of my life.

> From Michael's Letter to Mama,
> *More Tales of the City* by Armistead Maupin

If sex roles are the stubborn dandelion root of trouble
in the families of lesbians, gay men, and their parents,
Freudian theory on the cause of homosexuality is the

---

*A shortened version of this chapter was published in *The
Advocate*, Issue 392, April 17, 1984.

fertilizer that feeds that root. Freudian and neo-Freudian theory sends a uniquely personal message to parents, a message that has a devastating impact on our relationships.

When a daughter or son comes out, parents struggle to reconcile three conflicting ideas. Each idea is independent of the others, yet the three fit together like a set of Chinese boxes. The outer box contains an assimilation of homosexuality's negative image. The middle box is filled with the parents' dreams and hopes for a child who is now known to be homosexual. The smallest box, the core, holds the belief that parents cause their children to be homosexual. Each box conceals the next, but it is the innermost box, the one that contains the guilt, that must be opened first in order to reconcile the conflicts hidden in the other two. And it is that small box which is the most difficult for parents to open.

Even though, as we have seen, new research challenges the notions that parents' personalities or the ways in which parents related to their young children are major determinants of the sexual orientation of their children, many people still believe that bad mothers and fathers raise homosexual children. The twin negatives of homosexuality-as-disease and parents as the cause of that disease divide and alienate our families. A look at the origin of those ideas and how ingrained they have become explains why parents ask, "What did we do wrong?" The question reflects the blame built into the pathologic triangle of strong-mother-weak-father-homosexual-child.

Where the Guilt Came From

Early in the nineteenth century, the world of medicine mirrored the Bible's view of homosexuality as an evil practice that resulted from either insanity or degenerate willfulness, according to Ronald Bayer in *Homosexuality and American Psychiatry*. Later in the century, environmental, or nurturing, factors were claimed as contributing to what was then seen as an inherited predisposition for homosexuality.[1]

An ideological shift from the perception of homosexuality-as-evil to homosexuality-as-disease had, however, occurred by the turn of the century. Bayer confirmed that

> For Freud, as for most of those who undertook the scientific study of sexuality in the last years of the nineteenth century and the first years of the twentieth century, there was no question but that heterosexuality represented the normal end of psychosexual development.[2]

In addition to the bias of that view, Sigmund Freud himself acknowledged that his sexual theories were "based entirely upon everyday medical observation" (*not* on a scientific analysis of broad-based statistics), and that he had treated "only a single type of invert [homosexual] . . . whose sexual activity is in general stunted and the residue of which is manifested as inversion," (*not* mentally healthy individuals).[3] Despite such a flawed foundation, Freud's theories became the dominant force behind psychiatric thinking; they remain a major influence today.

One of those theories, the Oedipus complex,[4] taken from the myth of Oedipus who killed his father and married his mother, was considered by Freud as the base of all sexual and personality development. According to Freud, a boy became heterosexual when his mother was an affectionate care-taker who directed his choice towards women and his competitive father deflected him from his own sex.[5] Although Freud thought homosexuality resulted from a complex combination of both nature and nurture,[6] he believed that parents bore the primary responsibility for a faulty resolution of his Oedipus complex that resulted in a homosexual child. Both parents were at fault according to Freud, but he assigned the pivotal, active responsibility to the mother.[7]

To illustrate, Freud, who, of course, never knew either Leonardo da Vinci or his mother, boldly held her responsible for her famous son's homosexuality in this fanciful vignette.

> [Leonardo's] illegitimate birth deprived him of his father's influence until perhaps his fifth year, and left him open to the tender seductions of a mother whose only solace he was. After being kissed by her into precocious sexual maturity, he must no doubt have embarked on a phase of infantile sexual activity. . . .[8]

Dr. C. A. Tripp, psychologist and author, effectively satirized Freud's mother of a gay son in his book *The Homosexual Matrix*. The mother, said Tripp, was guilty if she behaved seductively towards her male child or, in other words, if she loved too much. She was also culpable if she were judged by others to dominate or over-protect her young son. Yet, she erred too if she treated him meanly or rejected him or, in other words, if she loved too little.[9] No mother, with or without a gay son, is immune to the contradictions and subjective value judgments of Freud's pathologic view of the cause of homosexuality.

Fathers contributed too, Freud said, in the making of homosexual sons, although he assigned them only passive responsibility. "The absence of a strong father in childhood," he wrote, "not infrequently favors the occurrence of inversion."[10] Freud's guilty father, then, might have been either a weakling who failed to provide an adequate male role model for his son or one who was absent altogether. The idea said two things: that it was necessary to *teach* boys about heterosexuality and that heterosexual men were masculine while gay men were something else.

Guilt Was Nurtured

Following Freud's lead, the world of psychotherapy nurtured the idea of parental guilt. A never-ending fascination with the etiology of homosexuallity blended conveniently with what became the popular practice of blaming mothers for all the problems of their children. Through the years the original pathologic theory was changed or elaborated by neo-Freudians to cover its inconsistencies.

An example of this was a study, now twenty years old, by psychoanalyst Irving Bieber, who not only upheld but embellished Freud's theories of parental guilt.[11] The conclusions in his study were based on information supplied by gay sons who were in analysis. In other words, Bieber's data on parents was not only not supplied by parents but was supplied by sons who were unhappy enough to be undergoing treatment. Furthermore, much of the information was secondhand. The sons confided in their analysts who, in turn, confided in Bieber; neither Bieber nor the others talked to the parents of their patients.[12]

Dr. Fritz Fluckiger, who subjected the Bieber study to a lengthy and careful analysis, denounced it as "bad science from start to finish," and concluded that Bieber's pathologic stance was based on "moral judgments which are disguised as clinical observations."[13]

In 1979 Bieber and an associate attempted to overcome criticism of his earlier methodology with a second study. Once again, his subjects were patients, gay men seeking help with their problems. He stated, too, that "about 100 pairs of parents" were "examined."[14] But as psychiatrist Michael Myers pointed out, "they do not explain how they 'examined' the parents."[15] Also, Bieber made no mention of a parental control group, a group of parents, for example, with troubled sons who were *heterosexual.* Such a comparison would have given essential relativity to the study. Not surprisingly, Bieber claimed his new data supported his earlier conclusions.

Despite the important challenge Alfred Kinsey posed as early as 1948 to both the insistence on pathologic family histories and the psychopathic understanding of homosexuality,[16] and despite the interesting fact that no one accuses parents of "causing" heterosexual children, the Freudian indictment of parents continues to be spouted by both nonexperts and others who should know better. It was, and still is, often presented in the form of advice on how *not* to raise children, presumably directed to those who are not yet parents or to parents of very young children.

About twenty years ago, for example, when my own children were small, one slick magazine with an immense circulation warned mothers against sowing "seeds of catastrophe" which could lead to "feminized" sons. The mother in the article was guilty of, among other things, running her fingers through her son's hair and addressing him endearingly.[17] No wonder the mother of a son in this book felt guilty. She blamed herself for her son's sexual orientation because, in his words, "She had shown me a lot of affection when I was younger."

A more recent example of mother as the guilty party was a statement by author Clinton Jones that "there is this drive in the mother [of a gay son] to find some way of taking the blame."[18] Nonsense! There is no such inherent maternal drive. The "drive" is something thrust upon mothers by the high authority of Freud and his disciples.

Similarly, mothers are also commonly blamed for their children's drug and alcohol abuse, their unsocial behavior, and something else called "the silent consequences," a dark state that results according to an overly dramatic male author when mother's "victims are so broken in spirit that they are not capable of deviation or dramatic action."[19]

Even feminist Betty Friedan parroted the sexist view of maternal guilt.

> The mother whose son becomes homosexual is usually not the "emancipated" woman who competes with men in the world, but the very paradigm of the feminine mystique—a woman who lives through her son, whose femininity is used in virtual seduction of her son. . . .[20]

Contradictorily, however, today's emancipated mother is warned that nontraditional, nonsexist parenting will also result in homosexual sons. It is, according to Judith Arcana, author of a book on mothering sons, "a classic case of damned if you do and damned if you don't; the blaming of mothers for male homosexuality is all-encompassing."[21]

Both parents are vituperatively identified in a book called *Growing Up Straight*. Lacking personal qualification to address the subject, the authors relied on the bias of case histories, quotations, and statistics from Irving Bieber to conclude that "children who become homosexual are singled out by an unhealthy parent in an unhealthy way."[22]

Another case of unwarranted guilt induction was found in a review of Alan Bell's and Martin Weinberg's *Homosexualities, A Study of Diversity Among Men and Women*, a book which does *not* deal with the causes of homosexuality. The reviewer, however, made the blatant, unrelated statement that *he* had "little doubt that homosexuality is almost always the result of parental inadequacy."[23] One can only hope no homosexual offspring had the misfortune to be born to these writers.

Again, in a recent instance, a widely-read columnist told her readers that a male child "who was born OK but becomes a homosexual usually identifies with his mother rather than his father."[24] Implicit parental blame was delivered in the morning paper and swallowed by millions of readers along with their scrambled eggs and toast.

These quotations come not from medical journals or obscure publications but from mainstream books, magazines, and newspapers. They all insist on viewing homosexuality as a sickness caused by parents. Unfortunately, such value-laden judgments have become a part of our society's store of general information. They are uniquely and devastatingly personal to parents of lesbian daughters and gay sons.

The Effect

To better understand the hurtful impact psychiatry has had on parents and the family, it is important to consider how long the pathologic view of parents has existed. As we have learned, the shift of the characterization of homosexuality from an inherited evil to a sickness was complete by the early 1900s; Freud's major theories on sexuality were published in 1905. Not until 1973, however, was homosexuality removed from the American Psychiatric Association's list of mental illnesses.

Considering, then, the slowness with which ideological change is accepted by the general population and proposing a twenty-year parent-child generation cycle, it becomes clear that all parents who are alive today have been indoctrinated to one degree or another with the idea that their "mistakes" could cause their child to be homosexual.

As a result, many parents have a knee-jerk reaction to their daughter's or son's disclosure: What did we do wrong? But as psychologist George Weinberg, pointed out, "Parents are not constructed by nature to shun homosexual children," and furthermore . . .

> Were it not for the mental health experts, millions of parents would be making independent decisions about their children's homosexuality, and many would decide that our national customs and laws here are unduly punitive. In other words, the mental health experts have cut down sharply the number of parents who rally to the side of their homosexual children.[25]

One vulnerable parent, Mary Borhek, who *did* rally to the side of her gay son, described in her first book, *My Son Eric,* how she felt when she applied the Irving Bieber models of "close-binding" mothers and "detached" fathers to herself and her former husband.

> I went downtown to the Minneapolis Public Library and got Dr. Bieber's book. It was not a book one would expect to curl up with and read avidly on a long winter evening. Nevertheless, I did. . . . Here was a psychiatrist, trained and knowledgeable, who had made huge samplings. He was not a woman deserted by her husband.
>
> As I read Bieber's book, there were many times when I cringed . . . not that either Tom or I had perpetrated the excesses detailed in Bieber's book. . . . Still, there were

a number of faint echoes of our family life
here and there in Bieber's book. Tom had
not made Eric a homosexual, nor had
I—alone. It had been like two muddy streams
flowing together. There was no possible way
these two could join forces and produce a
sparkling clear river.[26]

Such painful internalization of guilt was also a common
thread in the stories of those who contributed to this book.
Parents blamed themselves or one another . . .

(mD) I didn't know what I had done, but I
felt responsible.

* * * * *

(mD) I was very upset, and I thought, "Well,
what did I do wrong?" because, let's
face it, we were taught this is very bad.

* * * * *

(mD) I used to think if I'd made her wear
dresses more. . . .

* * * * *

(D) My mom thinks she shouldn't have let
me stay in my room so much. She
should have encouraged me to have
more male friends.

* * * * *

(D) That night my father sent me into the house. We had been looking at my car, and he said, "Now after you go home, it's up to your mother and me to figure out just what part we played in all this."

* * * * *

(S) To be honest, I think my mother feels like it's my father.

* * * * *

(S) My stepfather doesn't think he's responsible. He thinks my father is.

* * * * *

(S) I've heard my mother blame my father for it, saying that he never paid any attention to us, to the kids, and it was his fault and then . . . my father never says anything. He doesn't answer.

In addition to guilt, the Freudian notion has a paralyzing, secondary effect on parents. So long as parents accept as true even some small part of it, they remain unwilling to identify themselves as parents of lesbian daughters and gay sons. They hide from relatives and neighbors, and, inadvertently, they isolate themselves.

The price of isolation is high. It is painfully lonely. It also closes the door to help and stifles growth.

Six years after her daughter's disclosure, one mother

said, "I have a friend who I suspect also has a gay daughter, but we don't talk about it. It's sad because it would be nice to be able to talk to someone, especially since my husband and I don't talk about it. But I'm not going to say anything to my friend until she says something to me."

There is yet another unhappy consequence to the odious concept of homosexuality as a disease caused by parents. It encourages gay adults to reconstruct their past experiences in terms of Hostile-Detached Fathers and Dominant-Smothering Mothers. One of the sons in this book, for example, admitted that in anger he sometimes said, "Yes, Mother, you've made me this way," and, he added, "She gets very upset." Another son, who accused his father of "not ever having had any time to be with me," acknowledged that he made the connection between his own sexual orientation and his father's inaccessibility.

Not surprisingly, Kinsey Institute researchers Alan Bell, Martin Weinberg, and Sue Kiefer Hammersmith found that gay men and women who were familiar with psychoanalytic theory about homosexuality were much more likely to describe their parents according to theoretical stereotypes than were those unfamiliar with it.[27] And psychologist C. A. Tripp identified a self-perpetuating link between theory and reality. Unless therapists have, Tripp said,

> ... already earned a reputation for accepting homosexuality (or at least leaving it alone) they will seldom get the kind of clients for whom it is working at all well ... a far greater hazard is that most of the patients they do get are quite familiar with psychiatric ideas and have already translated their self-interpretations into these terms. ... Thus, one patient after the other presents a history

of having a dominant mother, a weak or
inattentive father, a package of early in-
securities, and all the rest.[28]

In short, biased research data and theoretical inconsistencies and contradictions aside, the pathologic view of
parents as the cause of homosexuality is still widely
believed. Freud's dominant mother and weak father have
become a pervasive part of our culture, the trolls of
psychiatry. The very imprecision of the Freudian and
neo-Freudian categories of parental guilt encourages their
continued application. The theory allows the unsophisticated
to feel smug, to play doctor. It makes the parents of young
children nervous and self-conscious. How much love is
enough love? It allows lesbian daughters and gay sons to
blame their parents. It creates massive guilt, emotional pain,
and self-imposed isolation for parents.

New Challenges

When I was the newly-aware mother of a gay son, I too
thought I had done something wrong. A wiser mother said
to me, "Don't spend your energy trying to figure out what
caused Jason to be gay. You'll need that energy to help
him live in our hostile society." That good advice helped
me in the beginning. Later, I began to question the validity
of the theory that pointed its finger at me.

A hole appeared in that theory when I tried to apply it
to my own family. Jason's father and I had tried our best
to be loving, supportive parents in pretty much equal
measures to both our children; however, even if we were
willing, in the interest of understanding our son, to take
on the strong-mother-weak-father roles that supposedly
account for his homosexual orientation, how could we
explain our heterosexual daughter?

Daughters, then, provided a challenge. The pathologic family perspective, consistently and almost exclusively applied to gay males, could logically, it would seem, be turned inside out like a dirty sock to a weak-mother-strong-father dynamic that would account for lesbianism. Freud, however, did not explain lesbianism by such a logical reversal of the factors he thought caused male homosexuality.

Instead, he offered more contradictory and sexist explanations. One lesbian, "a beautiful and clever girl of eighteen," was indeed diagnosed by Freud as having developed a deep antipathy to men because of her father's sternness. Earlier in the case history, however, Freud had described the same stern father as not only earnest and worthy but very tender hearted.[29] Freud exhibited no such deference to the mother in another of his case histories. She was accused by Freud of creating a "powerful emotional attachment" or a "homosexual bond" with her daughter that made it impossible for the young woman to love a man.[30]

The fact is that Freud and other theoreticians have had relatively little to say about lesbianism and what they have said is contradictory. For instance, the results of one study linked lesbianism to "unsatisfactory relations between the girl and her weak and incompetent father," not the strong, domineering father of the dirty-sock theory.[31]

Betty Friedan even absolved fathers from responsibility because, she theorized, a father, unlike a mother, "is not as often tempted or forced by society to live through or seduce his daughter."[32]

Yet another source stated that "the 'intolerable conflicts' that dispatch daughters into homosexuality tend to be set off by mothers. Usually these are domineering women: excessively bossy and hypercritical."[33]

All of these sources agree on only one thing: parents

"cause" lesbianism. Reproachful as the judgments are, they remain inconclusive and unconvincing. They are also all clearly reliant on Freud's theory. The imprecision, however, with which that theory is reversed to account for lesbianism, the unwillingness of the so-called experts to apply the same blame to fathers of lesbians that is unflinchingly applied to mothers of gay sons is a serious flaw in the theory. Also, the very adaptability of the theory to almost any maternal personality discounts its validity.

Furthermore, thoughtful researchers have also begun to question the Freudian mindset. While studies do continue to find many of our early relationships to be troubled, researchers are now more cautious in drawing conclusions from such findings. They are also alert to the fallacy of conclusions based on studies of mentally unhealthy individuals.

For example, one researcher, who had reviewed a group of both patient and nonpatient studies of gay males, concluded that "disturbed parental relations are neither necessary nor sufficient conditions for homosexuality to emerge."[34] Another researcher, who studied the parental backgrounds of both lesbians and gay sons, found that when he examined individuals who were mentally healthy, "differences in the parental backgrounds of homosexuals compared to heterosexuals were sharply reduced."[35]

In addition, the previously mentioned Bell, Weinberg, Hammersmith study disputes nearly all the developmental myths that surround homosexuality, and the authors of that study speak directly to our concerns.

> ... people who criticize the parents of homosexuals for what they view as an aberration will have no cause to lay blame on them, while parents of gays may be relieved of whatever guilt they may have felt about

their parenting. There is a growing consensus,
to which our own data lend support, that
not much can be predicted about an individual on the basis of his or her parental
relationships. While this consensus may
alienate those who have long thought otherwise, it may be reassuring to parents who
are discomfited by the fact that their children
are not carbon copies of themselves. . . .[36]

It is indeed comforting to parents to be found more or
less not guilty by the people who are held up as experts. It
is also comforting to see small signs that the judgmental
intensity of the Freudian theory may be weakening. In her
second book called *Coming Out to Parents*, Mary Borhek
rejects her own earlier acceptance of Bieber's guilt assign-
ment.

In my own case I knew immediately *why*
Eric is gay: *It was because of the home in
which he had grown up*. A number of years
and a good bit of information later I know it
was not my husband's or my fault, that the
causes of a same-sex orientation are complex.[37]

In conclusion, then, many mothers and fathers of
lesbian and gay children stumble over heavy guilt and
isolate themselves because they believe they caused their
children to be something bad. A vast amount of information,
both written and spoken, continues to reinforce that idea.

The guilt originated in the world of psychiatry which
first identified homosexuality as a sickness. Next, it set
about curing that sickness by finding its cause. Parents

became guilty by association; they were said to cause their child's sickness.

Today, however, thirty-five years after Kinsey first proposed the idea, homosexuality is understood by informed people to be only one variant of human sexuality, just a single component of a sexual continuum that ranges from exclusive heterosexuality to exclusive homosexuality and is connected by all the possible variations in between.[38] As such, it is no longer considered a sickness, and the search for its cause is becoming a broader search to understand the roots of all human sexuality. These truths reject the guilt imposed on parents of gay and lesbian children by psychiatry.

As mothers and fathers accept the naturalness of all their children's sexual orientations, and as they come to see that Freudian and neo-Freudian theory was based on inadequate numbers of mentally ill people, that it was frequently unchecked by control groups, that it was sexist, and that it contained illegitimate value judgments and contradictions, they will be able to open the smallest of the Chinese boxes and turn out the guilt that separates parent from child.

* * * * *

"It's your mother. I think she wants to cut off all diplomatic ties again."

CHAPTER 10

THEM AND US

MA   You haven't spoken a sentence since I got here without the word "Gay" in it.

ARNOLD Because that's what I am.

MA   If that were all you could leave it in there [Points to bedroom] where it belongs; in private. No, you're obsessed with it. You're not happy unless everyone is talking about it. . . .

ARNOLD [Bordering on hysteria] I don't know what to say to you. I really don't. I'm not trying to throw it in your face but it is what I am and it's not just a matter of who I sleep with. . . . Ma, try to imagine the world the other way around. Imagine that every movie, book, magazine, T.V. show, newspaper, commercial, billboard told you that you should be homosexual. But you know you're not and you know that for you this is right . . .

From the play *Torch Song Trilogy*
by Harvey Fierstein

139

Is homosexuality anti-family? TV evangelists, among others, insist it is. I believe, however, that saying homosexuality is anti-family is like saying trees are anti-forest. Trees, like children, come in different shapes, sizes, and colors, but the forest is no more threatened by the individual tree than the family is threatened by the homosexual child.

The truth is, homosexuality is much less anti-family than families are anti-homosexual. "Nowhere," according to Dr. Bruce Voeller, "has the hostility to homosexuality been more frightening to large numbers of gay men and lesbians than in their own families, forcing them to feel like minority group members in their own homes."[1]

The distance created by that hostility was not only familiar to the sons and daughters I interviewed for this book, but it remained a continuing source of despair. When asked how they would most like their relationships with their parents to be, this is what they said.

(D)   I wish there were more walls that weren't there.

* * * * *

(S)   I would like my mother to come to gay affairs, to pick up [a gay newspaper] and see what's going on. I'd like her to realize that discrimination doesn't stop with women, gays or blacks. I mean, it's all one, and I want her to recognize that she can really help a lot of her friends just by her attitudes. You know, it's a chain process.

* * * * *

(D)   I would like to be able to invite them here for dinner. I don't feel I could have them here. My mother has come to various apartments of mine alone or with my brothers and sisters, but my father has not.

* * * * *

(D)   I would love for them to be out to their family and friends . . . that would be fabulous.

* * * * *

(S)   I would be totally thrilled if my mother could just at some time or another integrate the fact that I'm gay into everything else that she knows about me.

* * * * *

(D)   What I know I like that I don't get is acknowledgment of my relationship with my lover and some validation for that. After seven years, my parents still see it as kind of a temporary thing.

* * * * *

(S)   I wish they would be able to accept me and my lover fully, that they'd be comfortable to have both of us over.

In an important sense, parents of lesbian daughters and gay sons decide whether or not homosexuality is anti-family. When parents hold back their approval or attach conditions to their love for their gay children, they create families of *them* and *us*.

What If A Parent Says, "Don't Come Home Again"?

Parents do reject their children. I learned that truth from my mother. In her eyes I had been an inconvenient child who grew into a toublesome adolescent. At sixteen I was thrown out of the house and out of her life. As an adult, I spent years seeking some magic combination of behavior, attitude, and accomplishments that would enable my mother to look at me and say, "You're a good daughter, after all. I love you." Instead, at her choice we are again estranged. I have learned to accept the absence of my mother and her approval as facts of my life. Furthermore, I have learned to separate my mother's view of me from the person I know myself to be.

Many of the daughters and sons in this book were also learning to make that difficult distinction. It is difficult because a child with limited reasoning powers and lack of experience understands and internalizes parental disapproval as a global truth. Even as adult daughters and sons, the experience of parental rejection is both sharp and long-lasting; it attacks our roots, our essence.

Three daughters and two sons had known a level of disapproval and rejection from their parents that resulted in long-term estrangement. All but one had attempted reconciliations that had not lasted.

One of the daughters, whose disclosure to her mother escalated into an angry exchange and, finally, estrangement, said, "My immediate reaction after my mother rejected me was terrible. I was really pretty devastated and became suicidal. I was in very bad shape for a very long time." However, with the perspective of three years, she said,

> I'm glad I got through my anger towards my mother. . . . I'm really glad that I told her who I was and what I felt and what my experience had been and really cleared the air with her. It was very painful, but I'm not sure it could have been really great no matter when I did it.

Surprisingly, none of those whose parents' rejection had resulted in estrangement regretted having come out to their parents. These are their stories.

(S)   I thought I'd tell my folks, and it would be all right, but it wasn't. I knew they wouldn't accept it, but I didn't think it would come to these ends. And yet I'm not sorry I told them. Why should I conform to a way that I'm not and be unhappy when I can just be myself and be happy? I would be so unhappy if I was still out in the suburbs living under their roof, being forced to date women or whatever. So, I'm happy that I've come out.

* * * * *

(D)   The honesty was most important. It's a burden lifted to be able to tell your parents. Whether they accept or not, there's relief that they understand where you're coming from. That's my opinion. . . .

Just before I stopped seeing my mother again the second time, we were sitting in the bedroom, and I told her, "All I ever wanted from you was to love me. That's all I ever wanted from you." She started to cry. She took me by the head, and pulled me to her body, and said, "I'm sorry." I realized at that moment, that very moment, that I had wanted her love so badly and when she was really trying to express it to me, I felt nothing. I realized I didn't love my mother, and I never would. I feel pity for her, but I don't feel love. That's just the way it is. It was just like a rush at that moment . . . and it relieved me. It was a relief that I could actually accept it.

* * * * *

(S) There was no relationship after my mother knew I was gay. Years passed before we even looked in each other's faces, let alone had a telephone call or a letter. Then for two years I had tried to salvage something as an adult man, not a homosexual, but as an adult man with an elderly mother. It was very painful. I saw it as being kind of hopeless. Both my therapist and my lover said, "You want your mother to be something that she'll never be, and that's much too frustrating for you." I agree with that. I wanted her to be a mother. I wanted her to put her arms around me and tell me that she loved me without there being a reason to do it. And I wasn't getting that.

I decided that I wanted nothing to do with my mother because it's not good for *me* emotionally. I began to slip back. I had progressed, emotionally, to a ten, and in the two years that I spent with her, I may have slipped back to a seven. She was extremely destructive.

* * * * *

(D) No, I don't wish I hadn't told my mother, not at all, but I didn't expect her to be as rejecting as she in fact was. I expected her to accept me. I expected it to be difficult, but I really believed in this fantasy of our family as a loving, together unit. . . .

Ideally, it seems like you work this stuff out and then you have some sort of a relationship. I no longer think that we are going to have a satisfying, good, comfortable relationship. I used to think that we'd work it out, and we'd come to something. I don't believe that any more. I still think it *may* be we can get to the point where we can be in the same room together and not have it be horribly painful or horribly enraging so that we can have family gatherings, but I'm not sure whether we'll ever get to that point or not.

I'm in the process of separating . . . every year I make more progress and now there are a few last stages of me wanting her approval, wanting something from her. But I'm almost completely finished with that to where I'm really separate. I feel best in a sense when I'm just angry at her, and I think of her as a total creep, you know? Then when something happens that seems genuine or nice or seems like she's trying, it hurts. It makes me feel bad. So, I honestly don't know where it's going to go.

Sometimes I think that, yeah, we should get together in a therapy session and sometimes I think that's a really stupid idea. I go back and forth. My sister said to me, "Gee, why don't you bury the hatchet with Mom? You're missing all this time you could be enjoying her." And I said to my sister, "I don't think I'll ever enjoy my mother." I think that's an impossibility. My greatest hope is that we might get to some neutral ground.

I believe the parent-child relationship deserves every

chance. Both generations are shortchanged when it breaks down.

I also know that the parent-child relationship can be destructive. In truth, some parents and children are better off apart. In families where the conflict is both deep-rooted and long-lasting and where minds are closed, daughters and sons are wise to put their energies into building other relationships that offer them comfort.

A woman contacted me while I was working on this chapter. She, too, was the mother of a gay son. Several unhappy years after her son had come out to her, he had given her an ultimatum—either she invite both him and his lover home for a visit, or he was not coming home again. The mother's dilemma came from an earlier ultimatum. She had told her son, "I can accept your homosexuality, but I can never accept your *practice* of homosexuality."

That mother and I talked a long time. These are some of the things I said to her: You may continue to defend your position, and assuredly, you will find others who agree with you. The outcome, however, will be the loss of your son. Even if he remains in your life, you will lose his spontaneity, his insight, and his joy at being with you.

Instead, I urged, please talk to your son. Help him to see that ultimatums only close down options. Tell him that you are giving yourself permission to rethink the position you have taken, and you hope he will do the same. Both your position and your son's position are based on strong principles. Sometimes, though, we are unable to live with the consequences of our principles, and it is important to remember that principles are, after all, just ideas, ideas that can change.

In conclusion, we are the only mothers and fathers our lesbian daughters and gay sons will ever have. Whatever our past disagreements, whatever differences we have now, we

148

must all take care not to confine our love to the facts of our lives but to let it go beyond those facts.

* * * * *

Untitled Work by artist, Kara Barnard. All Rights Reserved, The Naiad Press, Inc.

CHAPTER 11

MAKING IT WORK TOGETHER

My son took me by the hand and became a bridge to a place
where my own sensibilities were enlarged.

Ann Greene,
Mother of a gay son

Someday a well-known couple will give us a gift. They
will let it be known in a positive way that one of their
children is gay. I thought of such an event when I asked
the daughters and sons in this book, "How do you think
your parents would react if the President and First Lady
held a press conference to announce that their son was gay
and that they not only loved him but thought that having a
gay son enriched their lives?" I loved the answers.

(S) Oh, God, wouldn't that be great? Wouldn't that be wonderful? I'm sure that it would be good for my parents. I think that they'd probably say, "Well, we feel the same way about *our* son."

* * * * *

(D) My mother would probably think that was terrific . . . I think she needs to know that there are more people around.

* * * * *

(S) They'd say, "Why are they having a press conference? We've been loving our son for years. Is there something good on television?"

* * * * *

(D) Mom wouldn't like it. It would be like, "It's no one's business, so they have no business being on television talking about it." Dad would probably agree with that.

* * * * *

(S) I think they would consider it a little tacky, but they would relate it to their own experience.

* * * * *

(D)   They might take a look at my lesbianism
       a little bit differently and maybe try
       and find something that has enriched
       their life through it.

* * * * *

(S)   I think that would be the most wonder-
       ful thing that could happen. These are
       not people my mother particularly
       respects, but there's no question it
       would make her feel more comfortable.
       I think my mom is influenced by public
       opinion, and if it came down from on
       high that it was okay in America to be
       gay and to have a gay son, there's no
       question but that it would be a positive
       influence.

* * * * *

(D)   Well, my father is very much an advocate
       of the President. He would react nega-
       tively, and, in private, probably think
       about it. Not so much because it's the
       President, but the fact that that man
       on television had the guts to get up and
       publicly make that announcement and
       the courage to say that it in fact helped
       him.

Parents answered the question, too.

(mS) Oh, I'd love it!

* * * * *

(fD) It might help me to discuss it more openly with my co-workers.

* * * * *

(mD) It wouldn't affect me in any way. No, I don't care what their son is, and I don't really care how they feel about it.

* * * * *

(mD) I seriously don't believe it would be necessarily beneficial. . . . Look at the kinds of support we had for the Equal Rights Amendment—President and Mrs. Carter, the Fords, Lady Bird Johnson, Alan Alda, etc., and still no ERA.

* * * * *

(mS) I'd feel good about that. I think that would be a monumental advance that will never happen.

* * * * *

(fS) The public would be more out and be more open about it. They would accept the gay society much better.

* * * * *

(mD) Oh, good, join the human race. I think unless you've had a child who is gay or lesbian, you miss a lot in humility and growing.

* * * * *

(mD) Well, I think it would be terrific if a President of the United States, regardless of what his name is, would have guts enough to do that.

Unlikely as it is that such an announcement will ever come from the White House, the responses to that hypothetical event illustrated its value to parents. "What we need," confirmed Ann Greene, counselor therapist and charter member of Chicago's parent support group, "are parents coming out who are authentically at ease, whole, and comfortable, parents who truly feel it's fine that their child is gay."[1]

Few of the parents in this book had reached such a positive place. As we have noted earlier, parents did not spontaneously progress through stages of ever-increasing acceptance and positivity. Some parents had made early leaps of love; some, particularly if they were parents of sons, had become more positive later.

Life-threatening experiences had also brought a few families closer. In one family, the tragedy of a son's struggle with AIDS, a story presented in an earlier chapter, illustrated the power of such an experience. In another family, a daughter said, "My mom was ill and almost died about a year ago. I think that was a real eye opener for her as well as for me. There were a lot of walls that were gone all of a sudden, a lot of reaching out and touching that had not been there." A series of heart attacks had prompted another mother to tell her son, "The thought of dying and leaving you with the memory I didn't love you or accept you was more than I could handle."

Other parents became more accepting after they had vented their negative feelings. The silent father of one son, for example, was provoked into anger three months after the disclosure. "My father," the son said, "just went nuts. He was very nasty, but after that things seemed to get better." Another parent, a mother of two gay sons, also thought expression of her early feelings had been helpful. "In the beginning," she said, "it was almost as if my sons had both died. I had such a sense of grief. I used to walk the floors at night and just wail, and I'd hold my mouth so my little girl upstairs wouldn't hear me. I was also angry. Being a grandmother was important to me, and I thought, 'They're denying me grandchildren!' " That same mother urged other parents to "get that hurt, that anger out. Get it behind you. Don't repress it. Do the crying, the screaming, whatever it takes to get it out."

The airing of such strong feelings, called catharsis, is a necessary first step for some parents. A parent's cathartic expression, on the other hand, is best not directed at a daughter or son. "Doing so," cautioned Greene, "places a tremendous burden upon the gay person, one that would require extreme, almost monumental maturity. If there's a need for cathartic expression of hostility and pain and fear, support groups, counseling, and therapy are very, very helpful because they relieve the burden on the family."[2]

Yet another experience, something I call "nudging," encouraged other parents to grow. More than a few daughters and sons refused to facilitate their parents' denial, because, as one daughter explained, "When I was trying to cover it up and protect my parents, they *allowed* that, but when I took the risk of being open, it forced them to be more accepting."

Nudging: What It Is and How It Works

Tom Sauerman, father of a gay son and leader of a parents' support group in Philadelphia, believes that parents need to learn from the experience of their gay children. "You may find," Sauerman says, "your parent-child roles reversed for a while."[3]

Jason had initiated such a reversal of roles in our family. When he came out to his father and me, he gave us the telephone number of the parents' group in Chicago. Several months later he asked if we had contacted the group. We had not. His response was, "I want you and Dad to go to that group, and I don't want you to go just once or twice. I want you to get involved." We went to the next meeting, or at least Jason and I did. Herman dropped us off that first time and went his own way. The second time, however, he came in with us.

Walking into that meeting took courage. It was our first public acknowledgment of a family situation we then wished did not exist. The people we met in the group, daughters and sons as well as other parents, welcomed us, listened to us, shared their own experiences, and, over the months and years that followed, challenged and stretched our thinking. Looking back, I am not sure we would have gone to the group had Jason not insisted on it.

Jason's insistence nudged or prodded us into growing. Other parents in this book had also grown as a result of having been nudged. Nudging was pressure applied to parents by daughters and sons to be open about homosexuality, to meet other gay people and other parents of gay people, to read, and to question. In short, nudging promoted the experiences that allowed parents to discard the negative myths and stereotypes surrounding homosexuality. Importantly, nudging led but did not shove.

Nudging recognized parents' feelings at the same time as it refused to accept arbitrary limits set by parents. Nudging pointed a new direction. It risked the status quo for something better.

One son told how, three years after telling his parents he was gay, he took advantage of an opportunity to nudge them.

One Sunday afternoon my parents had been invited to dinner at my apartment. Well, some friends of theirs, people I knew when I was growing up, were in town and had suggested that the four of them have dinner. My father didn't know what to do with that except to call me and ask was there enough dinner for all of us. I said, "Well, yes, there is; however, I don't intend to hide my lifestyle in order to accommodate your friends."

He said, "That means you won't put the magazines away and you won't do anything special?" I said, "No, and you won't either. When you walk in the front door, it's my house, and I am who I am." He kind of sighed deeply and turned around and asked if they'd like to join us for dinner.

I didn't go around and do anything different to my apartment; there was a copy of [a gay magazine] on the table. When they came, my father walked through the apartment. He picked up the magazine and thumbed through it and when he put it back down on the table, he put it back face down. I said, "Are you hiding something or

did you accidentally turn that face down?"
He said, "Okay," and turned it over.

Well, his friends were clever enough not to
ask what it was that he might be hiding, but
both of them worked their way over to the
table eventually, picked up the magazine,
leafed through it, and put it back down
without comment until about half way
through dinner.

Then the wife blurted out, "Well, are you a
homosexual or just your roommate?" My
mother kind of choked on whatever it was
she was eating, and I said, "Well, I am, of
course. I wouldn't have that magazine in my
house if I wasn't." And we had a very nice,
civil, intellectual discussion. One of her first
questions was, "Is it true that all gay people
live in San Francisco?" I said, "No, no, we
don't live in San Francisco. We live in
Denver and Houston and Chicago and Boston.
We *vacation* in San Francisco." That got a
laugh even from my parents.

Two other sons, whose mothers did not live in Chicago,
used two different forms of nudging over the telephone. The
first son explained,

I have an understanding with my mother. At
times I speak of my homosexuality. It's like,
"Okay, I'm gay, Mom," and that's the statement I'm making to you about whatever's
happening in my life right now." I called her
once on Gay Pride Day, and I said, "Happy
Gay Pride Day," cause I was feeling good

about myself and the day and everything. She said, "What's that?" and I said, "Oh, Mom, you know. We have a parade and it's sort of a celebration of our homosexuality." She said, "Oh, well, they don't have a parade here."

She doesn't necessarily approve of it, because she will refer to the Bible, stating that the Bible says this is wrong. Then it's up to me to make the next step to kind of hush her up. I'll go, "Yeah, Mom, I know, but it's how I *am*." It's a manipulative thing I do, and whether she truly understands me or not, I try to give her every opportunity to do that.

The second son said,

It's still pretty rosy when we are talking as long as we never talk about the fact that I had told her that I was gay, and I wanted to know what she thought about that. So, I sort of keep pushing it. I mean, maybe I'll drop it for a week or two but then I say, "Well, it's been several weeks, and we haven't talked about it. I want to know what you're thinking now."

I explained that one of the reasons I wanted to tell her that [I was gay] was because I wanted to start living my life like a full person, that I was tired of all the years I had already spent editing what was going on in my life and talking to her like some stranger. One of the things I explained is

that I really would like to get to the point
where if I'm seriously in a relationship with
someone, I want to be able to bring that
person home and have him accepted in the
same way that she would accept my sister's
boyfriends. In fact, I gave her that example.

Sometimes I'll talk to her about guys that
I'm dating. It's so easy for me to just say,
"Well, Bob and I went to Milwaukee last
weekend." She doesn't bristle, but she won't
really ask any questions. I'll needle her just
a little, like, "Well, you didn't even ask me
where he's from or where I met him. Don't
you care?" She'll answer, "Yeah, I know,
what's he like?" (laugh) She knows it's a
game, and she'll go along. If I never said
another word about it, I think that would
be the last I'd ever hear, but my mother
backs off less and less each time.

The next two illustrations of nudging came from daughters. The first daughter brought about her parents' acknowledgment of her relationship with a lover.

My feeling was if my parents got to know
Betty and liked her as a person that might
make it easier. Even though it was clear to
me they must have known the nature of the
relationship between Betty and me, it had
never been acknowledged that we were living
together. I felt a need to acknowledge it, so
I said, "I have not ever said that I'm
involved in a relationship with Betty, and
I'm very happy. The best part of my life is

my relationship with Betty. I feel like I can't share that with you, and I want to be able to do that. My fear is that you'd never invite Betty home for the holidays or whatever."

It was a real major change for my dad from where he was three and a half years ago. He said something empathetic which is the first time he'd ever done that in relation to this. He said, "I'm sure it has been very hard."

Since then we don't really talk about it directly, except they do ask about Betty ... how's she doing in school and at work, and they'll say, "When are you and Betty going on vacation?" There's more an acknowledgment of our relationship.

A second daughter described a lighthearted approach to nudging. She laughingly said,

I harrass my mother. I do. Stuff like, "Come on, Mom, come to MCC [Metropolitan Community Church, a gay congregation] with me." She'll say, "I already went to church." "That's okay," I tell her, "you can go twice. Just think how nice it would be if you went *twice*. Then you don't have to go next week." That kind of stuff.

Sometimes I kid her when I have a new friend over. I say, "I think she's cute. What do you think, Mom? Come on, Ma, do we have the same taste?"

> I've also given her books by Rita Mae
> Brown, and she reads them all, gives them
> back, and then we discuss the characters,
> who she's liked and who she hasn't liked
> and stuff like that.

Nudging parents requires skill and patience, and, like the disclosure, it is not a one-time effort but part of a process. Furthermore, nudging does not invariably result in increased parental understanding and acceptance. I believe, however, it is an essential ingredient to such growth. Parents do not grow by themselves.

Conclusion

In the final analysis, parents do indeed matter. Lesbian daughters, as women outside the social and financial security available to heterosexual women, need the recognition and approval of their parents. Gay sons, as men now threatened by devastating illness, need the recognition and approval of their parents. Both daughters and sons, as women and men harshly judged by the larger society, need and deserve the love and support of their families.

The relationships of lesbians, gay men, and their parents are uniquely complex, often troubled. We have built walls of rigid sex-role expectations. We have closed doors to hide the guilt and shame induced by the theories of others.

If our relationships are to improve, we must be wise enough and strong enough to reject the concepts behind those barriers. We parents, in particular, must be willing to re-evaluate old ideas and risk new ones in much the way our children have done before us. We must be willing to learn from our children, and they, in turn, must be willing to help us make such a re-evaluation.

If our relationships are to improve, we must stop being adversaries and become advocates instead. We must replace our shame with pride. Together we must pull down the walls and open the doors that separate us.

* * * * *

RESOURCES

Information on the nearest parent support group or parent contact is available from Parents FLAG, Box 24565, Los Angeles, CA 90024.

Free Pamphlets

Send a long, stamped, self-addressed envelope with each request.

About Our Children, Parents FLAG, Box 24565, Los Angeles, CA 90024.

Read This Before Coming Out to Your Parents, Parents of Gays, Box 15711, Philadelphia, PA 19103.

What Does the Bible Say About Homosexuality?, Good Shepherd Parish, Metropolitan Community Church, 615 W. Wellington, Chicago, IL 60657.

Nonfiction Books

Coming Out to Parents, A Two-way Survival Guide for Lesbians and Gay Men and Their Parents by Mary V. Borhek (New York: Pilgrim Press, 1983).

My Son Eric by Mary V. Borhek (New York: Pilgrim Press, 1979).

Now That You Know, What Every Parent Should Know About Homosexuality by Betty Fairchild and Nancy Hayward (New York: Harcourt Brace Jovanovich, 1979).

Are You Still My Mother? Are You Still My Family? by Gloria Guss Back (New York: Warner Books, 1985).

Beyond Acceptance, Parents of Lesbians and Gays Talk About Their Experiences by Carolyn Welch Griffin, Mirian J. and Arthur G. Wirth (Englewood Cliffs, NJ: Prentice-Hall, 1986).

Loving Someone Gay by Don Clark (Millbrae, CA: Celestial Arts, 1977).

Fiction Books

The Color Purple by Alice Walker (New York: Washington Square Press, reprint, 1983).

Tales of the City by Armistead Maupin (New York: Ballantine Books, reprint, 1979).

The Best Little Boy in the World by John Reid (New York: G. P. Putnam, 1973).

* * * * *

NOTES

Chapter 1. Who We Are

1. Ann Greene, Interview with author, Chicago, Illinois, 14 Dec. 1983.

2. George Weinberg, *Society and the Healthy Homosexual* (1972; reprint, New York: St. Martin's Press, 1983), 110.

3. May Sarton, *Journal of a Solitude* (New York: W. W. Norton, 1973), 91, referring to her novel, *Mrs. Stevens Hears the Mermaid Singing,* published in 1965.

4. Howard Brown, M.D., *Familiar Faces Hidden Lives, The Story of Homosexual Men in America Today* (New York: Harcourt Brace Jovanovich, 1976), 68.

5. Dr. Kinsey measured human sexuality on a six-point scale where point 0 represented exclusive heterosexuality and point 6 represented exclusive homosexuality. Points 1 and 2 were gradations of heterosexuality; point 3 was an even blend of heterosexuality and homosexuality; and

points 4 and 5 were gradations of homosexuality. The calculation in this chapter included the percent of individuals Kinsey rated 4 through 6 on the above scale together with the 1980 census population of 226,545,805.

6. Marcel T. Saghir and Eli Robins, *Male and Female Homosexuality, A Comprehensive Investigation* (Baltimore: Williams & Wilkins, 1973), 171; Karla Jay and Allen Young, *The Gay Report: Lesbians and Gay Men Speak Out About Sexual Experiences & Lifestyles* (New York: Summit Books, 1979), 68, 141.

7. Charles Silverstein, *A Family Matter, A Parents' Guide to Homosexuality* (1977; reprint, New York: McGraw-Hill paperback edition, 1978).

8. Federation of Parents & Friends of Lesbians and Gays, Inc., *About Our Children* (Los Angeles, 1982), 6. (To order this free pamphlet see information in Resources list.)

Chapter 2. Telling Parents

1. James Walters and Lynda Henley Walters, "The Role of the Family in Sex Education," *Journal of Research and Development in Education* 16, no. 2 (1983):8. (The Walterses also made the fascinating observation on page 9 that both generations underestimate the sexual behavior of the other.)

2. Vivienne C. Cass, "Homosexuality Identity Formation: A Theoretical Model," *Journal of Homosexuality* 4, no. 3 (Spring 1979):222.

Chapter 3. Parents' First Reactions

1. Karla Jay and Allen Young, *The Gay Report: Lesbians and Gay Men Speak Out About Sexual Experiences &*

Lifestyles (New York: Summit Books, 1979), 69, 143–144.

2. Thomas Garrett, "What Parents Know, A Convention of Mothers and Fathers," *New York Native,* 24 Oct.–6 Nov. 1983.

Chapter 4. How It Worked Out

1. Information from others who think parents *do* experience stages of growth may be found in: *Read This Before Coming Out to Your Parents,* a pamphlet by T. H. Sauerman, father of a gay son (to order see information in Resources list); *Beyond Acceptance, Parents of Lesbians and Gays Talk About Their Experiences,* a book by Carolyn Welch Griffin, Marian J. Wirth and Arthur G. Wirth, parents of gay sons (Englewood Cliffs, NJ: Prentice-Hall, 1986); and *Parents of the Homosexual* by David and Shirley Switzer, religious counselors (Philadelphia: Westminster Press, 1980).

2. See Resources list of nonfiction books.

3. Jean Seligmann, Mariana Gosnell, Vincent Coppola, and Mary Hager, "The AIDS Epidemic: The Search for a Cure," *Newsweek,* 18 Apr. 1983, 74–79.

4. Lawrence Bommer and Albert Williams, "AIDS Claims 2 Well-Known Chicago Gay Men," *Gaylife,* 11 Oct. 1984.

Chapter 5. A Closer Look

1. Norval D. Glenn and Charles N. Weaver, "Attitudes Toward Premarital, Extramarital, and Homosexual Relations in the 1970s," *Journal of Sex Research* 15, no. 2 (May 1979):117–118; Wainwright Churchill, *Homosexual Behavior Among Males, A Cross-Cultural and Cross-Species Investigation* (New York: Hawthorn Books, 1967), 155; Wardell B.

168

Pomeroy, *Dr. Kinsey and the Institute for Sex Research* (New York: Harper and Row, 1972), 67.

2. Stephen F. Morin and Ellen M. Garfinkle, "Male Homophobia," *Journal of Social Issues* 34, no. 1 (1978):35; John Dunbar, Marvin Brown, and Donald M. Amoroso, "Some Correlates of Attitudes Toward Homosexuality," *Journal of Social Psychology* 89 (1973):278; Eugene E. Levitt and Albert D. Klassen, Jr., "Public Attitudes Toward Homosexuality: Part of the 1970 National Survey by the Institute for Sex Research," *Journal of Homosexuality* 1, no. 1 (Fall 1974):41; William L. Yarber and Bernadette Yee, "Heterosexuals' Attitudes toward Lesbianism and Male Homosexuality: Their Affective Orientation toward Sexuality and Sex Guilt," *Journal of American College Health* 31, no. 5 (April 1983):207.

3. Morin and Garfinkle, 31; Knud S. Larsen, Rodney Cate, and Michael Reed, "Anti-Black Attitudes, Religious Orthodoxy, Permissiveness, and Sexual Information: A Study of the Attitudes of Heterosexuals Toward Homosexuality," *Journal of Sex Research* 19, no. 2 (May 1983):111–112.

4. Patrick Irwin and Norman L. Thompson, "Acceptance of the Rights of Homosexuals: A Social Profile," *Journal of Homosexuality* 3, no. 2 (Winter 1977):113; Knud S. Larsen, Michael Reed, and Susan Hoffman, "Attitudes of Heterosexuals Toward Homosexuality: A Likert-Type Scale and Construct Validity," *Journal of Sex Research* 16, no. 3 (Aug. 1980):252.

5. Kenneth L. Nyberg and Jon P. Alston, "Analysis of Public Attitudes Toward Homosexual Behavior," *Journal of Homosexuality* 2, no. 2 (Winter 1976–77):101; Irwin and Thompson, 113; Glenn and Weaver, 117.

6. Nancy M. Henley and Fred Pincus, "Interrelationship of Sexist, Racist, and Antihomosexual Attitudes," *Psychological Reports* 42, no. 1 (Feb. 1978):86–87.

7. Levitt and Klassen, 41; L. M. Leitner and Suzana Cado, "Personal Constructs and Homosexual Stress," *Journal of Personality and Social Psychology* 43, no. 4 (1982):872.

8. Melvin L. Kohn, *Class and Conformity, A Study in Values* (Homewood, IL: Dorsey Press, 1969), 190.

9. Nyberg and Alston, 102; Irwin and Thompson, 114; Walter G. West, "Public Tolerance of Homosexual Behavior," *Cornell Journal of Social Relations* 12, no. 1 (Spring 1977):32; Rodney G. Karr, "Homosexual Labeling and the Male Role," *Journal of Social Issues* 34, no. 3 (1978):78; Henley and Pincus, 86; Glenn and Weaver, 114–115.

10. Morin and Garfinkle, 36; Ellen M. Garfinkle and Stephen F. Morin, "Psychologists' Attitudes toward Homosexual Psychotherapy Clients," *Journal of Social Issues* 34, no. 3 (1978):106–107; Terry Alan Sandholzer, "Physician Attitudes and Other Factors Affecting the Incidence of Sexually Transmitted Diseases in Homosexual Males," *Journal of Homosexuality* 5, no. 3 (Spring 1980):325–326.

11. See studies cited in Barry Glassner and Carol Owen, "Variations in Attitudes Toward Homosexuality," *Cornell Journal of Social Relations* 11, no. 2 (Fall 1976):163; and Levitt and Klassen, 41; Walter W. Hudson and Wendell A. Ricketts, "A Strategy for the Measurement of Homophobia," *Journal of Homosexuality* 5, no. 4 (Summer 1980):368.

12. Marilyn Yalom, Wenda Brewster and Suzanne Estler, "Women of the Fifties: Their Past Sexual Experiences and Current Sexual Attitudes in the Context of Mother/Daughter Relationships," *Sex Roles* 7, no. 9 (1981):885–886.

13. Levitt and Klassen, 41; Irwin and Thompson, 114–115; Gary L. Hansen, "Measuring Prejudice Against Homosexuality (Homosexism) Among College Students: A New Scale," *Journal of Social Psychology* 117, Second Half (Aug. 1982):236; G. Edward Stephan and Douglas R.

McMullin, "Tolerance of Sexual Nonconformity: City Size as a Situational and Early Learning Determinant," *American Sociological Review* 47, no. 3 (June 1982):411, 413.

14. Nyberg and Alston, 102; Gary L. Hansen, "Androgyny, Sex-Role Orientation, and Homosexism," *Journal of Psychology* 112, no. 1 (Sept. 1982):43; Stephan and McMullin, 411, 413.

15. Irwin and Thompson, 114–115.

16. Glassner and Owen, 169; Jim Millham, Christopher L. San Miguel, and Richard Kellogg, "A Factor-Analytic Conceptualization of Attitudes Toward Male and Female Homosexuals," *Journal of Homosexuality* 2, no. 1 (Fall 1976):8.

17. Nyberg and Alston, 102; Irwin and Thompson, 120.

18. See Gallup as cited in Morin and Garfinkle, 36; Glenn and Weaver, 115.

19. Levitt and Klassen, 41.

20. Larsen, Cate, and Reed, 111; Gregory K. Lehne, "Homophobia Among Men," in *The Forty-Nine Percent Majority: The Male Sex Role,* eds. Deborah S. David and Robert Brannon (Reading, MA: Addison-Wesley Publishing, 1976), 76; S. F. Morin and S. F. Wallace, "Religiosity, Sexism, and Attitudes Toward Homosexuality," Paper presented at meeting of California State Psychological Association, March, 1975, as cited in Morin and Garfinkle, 32; Henley and Pincus, 86–89.

21. Jason P. Muller, "Minority Status and Parents of Gays," (BA requirement, Kalamazoo College, 1983), 24.

22. Levels of parental appreciation and approval were assessed on a numbered scale that was applied by daughters and sons to two periods in their young lives, from ages seven to fourteen and from ages fourteen to twenty-one. The scale was applied separately to mothers and fathers, and all of the scores were then averaged to provide

definitions of positive or negative growing-up relationships with parents.

23. Alan P. Bell, Martin S. Weinberg, and Sue Kiefer Hammersmith, Chaps. 3, 4, 10, 11 in *Sexual Preference, Its Development in Men and Women* (Bloomington, IN: Indiana University Press, 1981).

24. Bell, Weinberg, Hammersmith, 191–192, 219.

25. Bell, Weinberg, Hammersmith, 124–125, 133, 54–55.

Chapter 6. Why Biological Sex Was So Important

1. Nina Lee Colwill, Judy Conn, and Hilary M. Lips, "Wives & Husbands, Mothers & Fathers," in *The Psychology of Sex Differences,* eds. Hilary M. Lips and Nina Lee Colwill (Englewood Cliffs, NJ: Prentice-Hall, 1978), 249.

2. Judith H. Langlois and A. Chris Downs, "Mothers, Fathers, and Peers as Socialization Agents of Sex-typed Play Behaviors in Young Children," *Child Development* 51, no. 4 (Dec. 1980):1245; Warren Farrell, *The Liberated Man, Beyond Masculinity: Feeling Men and Their Relationships with Women* (New York: Random House, 1974), 120; Jeanne Humphrey Block, "Conceptions of Sex Role: Some Cross-Cultural and Longitudinal Perspectives," *American Psychologist* 28, no. 6 (June 1973):517; Miriam M. Johnson, "Sex Role Learning in the Nuclear Family," *Child Development* 34 (1963):331.

3. Marc Feigen Fasteau, *The Male Machine* (New York: McGraw-Hill, 1974), 96.

4. Janet Saltzman Chafetz, *Masculine/Feminine or Human? An Overview of the Sociology of Sex Roles* (Itasca, IL: F. E. Peacock, 1974), 179.

5. Catherine S. Chilman, "Parent Satisfactions-

Dissatisfactions and Their Correlates," *Social Service Review* 53, no. 2 (June 1979):203.

6. Michael E. McGill, *The McGill Report on Male Intimacy* as excerpted in the *Chicago Tribune,* 18 June 1985.

7. Eleanor Emmons Maccoby and Carol Nagy Jacklin, *The Psychology of Sex Differences* (Stanford, CA: Stanford University Press, 1974):298.

8. R. Brown, *Social Psychology* (New York: Free Press, 1965), 161, as cited in Joseph H. Pleck, *The Myth of Masculinity* (Cambridge, MA: The MIT Press, 1981) 135.

9. Letty Cottin Pogrebin, *Growing Up Free, Raising Your Child in the 80's* (1980; reprint, New York: Bantam Books, 1981) 81.

10. Stephen F. Morin and Ellen M. Garfinkle, "Male Homophobia," *Journal of Social Issues* 34, no. 1 (1978):31; John Dunbar, Marvin Brown, and Donald M. Amoroso, "Some Correlates of Attitudes Toward Homosexuality," *Journal of Social Psychology* 89 (1973):278–279; A. P. MacDonald, Jr. and Richard G. Games, "Some Characteristics of Those Who Hold Positive and Negative Attitudes Toward Homosexuals," *Journal of Homosexuality* 1, no. 1 (Fall 1974):19–22; Gregory K. Lehne, "Homophobia Among Men," in *The Forty-Nine Percent Majority: The Male Sex Role,* eds. Deborah S. David and Robert Brannon (Reading, MA: Addison-Wesley Publishing, 1976) 76–77; Patrick Irwin and Norman L. Thompson, "Acceptance of the Rights of Homosexuals: A Social Profile," *Journal of Homosexuality* 3, no. 2 (Winter 1977):119; Dorothy I. Riddle and Barbara Sang, "Psychotherapy with Lesbians," *Journal of Social Issues* 34, no. 3 (1978):94; Gary L. Hansen, "Androgyny, Sex-Role Orientation, and Homosexism," *Journal of Psychology* 112, no. 1 (Sept. 1982):42–44, and other studies cited in those works.

11. Joseph Harry, *Gay Children Grown Up, Gender Culture and Gender Deviance* (New York: Praeger Publishers, 1982) 238.

12. Lehne, 78.

Chapter 7. Sex Roles: Parents and Sons

1. Letty Cottin Pogrebin, *Family Politics, Love and Power on an Intimate Frontier* (New York: McGraw-Hill, 1983), 203.

2. Alan P. Bell, Martin S. Weinberg, and Sue Kiefer Hammersmith, *Sexual Preference, Its Development in Men and Women* (Bloomington, IN: Indiana University Press, 1981), 60.

3. Don Clark, *Loving Someone Gay* (Millbrae, CA: Celestial Arts, 1977), 13.

4. Marc Feigen Fasteau, *The Male Machine* (New York: McGraw-Hill, 1974), 139.

5. Alan P. Bell and Martin S. Weinberg cite a higher incidence of marriage among lesbians than gay men and suggest some reasons why that might be true in *Homosexualities, A Study of Diversity Among Men and Women* (1978; reprint, New York: Simon and Schuster, 1979), 169–170.

Chapter 8. Sex Roles: Parents and Daughters

1. Alan P. Bell, Martin S. Weinberg, and Sue Kiefer Hammersmith, *Sexual Preference, Its Development in Men and Women* (Bloomington, IN: Indiana University Press, 1981), 124.

2. Eleanor Emmons Maccoby and Carol Nagy Jacklin,

The Psychology of Sex Differences (Stanford, CA: Stanford University Press, 1974), 312–327.

3. A. N. O'Connell as cited in Dorothy I. Riddle and Barbara Sang, "Psychotherapy with Lesbians," *Journal of Social Issues*, 34, no. 3 (1978):85–86.

4. B. E. Lott as cited in Letty Cottin Pogrebin, *Growing Up Free, Raising Your Child in the 80's* (1980; reprint, New York: Bantam Books, 1981), 149–150.

5. Nancy M. Henley and Fred Pincus, "Interrelationships of Sexist, Racist, and Antihomosexual Attitudes," *Psychological Reports* 42, no. 1 (Fall 1978):84.

Chapter 9. Why Parents Ask, "What Did We Do Wrong?"

1. Ronald Bayer, *Homosexuality and American Psychiatry, The Politics of Diagnosis* (New York: Basic Books, 1981), 18–19.

2. Bayer, 21.

3. Sigmund Freud, *Three Essays on the Theory of Sexuality,* ed. and trans. James Strachey (New York: Basic Books, 1962), xiv, lln.1.

4. Freud first mentioned the Oedipus complex in "The Interpretation of Dreams," *The Basic Writings of Sigmund Freud,* ed. and trans. A. A. Brill (New York: Modern Library, 1938), 308 (V.D.b).

5. Freud, *Three Essays,* 95.

6. Sigmund Freud, "The Psychogenesis of a Case of Homosexuality in a Woman," in *Sexuality and the Psychology of Love,* ed. Philip Rieff (1963; reprint, New York: Collier Books, 1968), 156–157.

7. Bayer, 24–25.

8. Sigmund Freud, *Leonardo da Vinci and a Memory of His Childhood,* translated by Alan Tyson, the Standard

Edition under general editorship of James Strachey (New York: W. W. Norton, 1964), 81–82.

9. C. A. Tripp, *The Homosexual Matrix* (1975; reprint, New York: Signet, 1976), 72–73.

10. Freud, *Three Essays,* 12n.1.

11. Irving Bieber, et al., *Homosexuality, A Psychoanalytic Study of Male Homosexuals* (New York: Basic Books, 1962).

12. Bieber, 25–29.

13. Fritz A. Fluckiger, "Research Through A Glass, Darkly, An Evaluation of the Bieber Study on Homosexuality," offprint from *The Ladder,* 10 (10, 11, 12, 1966), 21, 2.

14. Irving Bieber and Toby B. Bieber, "Male Homosexuality," *Canadian Journal of Psychiatry* 24, no. 5 (1979):409.

15. Michael F. Myers, "Counseling the Parents of Young Homosexual Male Patients," *Journal of Homosexuality* 7, nos. 2/3 (Winter/Spring 1981–1982):133.

16. Alfred C. Kinsey, Wardell B. Pomeroy, and Clyde E. Martin, *Sexual Behavior in the Human Male* (Philadelphia: W. B. Saunders, 1948), 315, 661; and *Sexual Behavior in the Human Female* with Paul H. Gebhard (1953), 19, 447.

17. Lester David, "Our Son Was Different," *Good Housekeeping,* Jan. 1966, 120, 122.

18. Clinton R. Jones, *Understanding Gay Relatives and Friends* (New York: Seabury Press, 1978), 11.

19. Hans Sebald, *Momism, The Silent Disease of America* (Chicago: Nelson Hall, 1976), 170.

20. Betty Friedan, *The Feminine Mystique* (New York: W. W. Norton, 1963), 275.

21. Judith Arcana, *Every Mother's Son, The Role of Mothers in the Making of Men* (Garden City, NY: Anchor Press/Doubleday, 1983), 172.

22. Peter and Barbara Wyden, *Growing Up Straight,*

176

What Every Thoughtful Parent Should Know About Homo-sexuality (New York: Stein and Day, 1968), 48.

23. Ashley Montagu, review of *Homosexualities, A Study of Diversity Among Men and Women,* by Alan P. Bell and Martin S. Weinberg, *Psychology Today,* Aug. 1978, 91.

24. Ann Landers, "Male Role Models Necessary to Raise Heterosexual Boy," *Chicago Sun-Times,* 7 July 1983.

25. George Weinberg, *Society and the Healthy Homo-sexual* (1972; reprint, New York: St. Martin's Press, 1983), 93, 94.

26. Mary V. Borhek, *My Son Eric* (New York: Pilgrim Press, 1979), 75, 76.

27. Alan P. Bell, Martin S. Weinberg, and Sue Kiefer Hammersmith, *Sexual Preference, Its Development in Men and Women* (Bloomington, IN: Indiana University Press, 1981), 20, 45n, 119n, 128n, 210–211.

28. Tripp, 235.

29. Freud, "A Case of Homosexuality in a Woman," 133, 135, 151.

30. Sigmund Freud, "A Case of Paranoia Running Counter to the Psychoanalytical Theory of the Disease," in *Sexuality and Psychology of Love,* 102.

31. Eva Bene, "On the Genesis of Female Homosexu-ality," *British Journal of Psychiatry* 111 (1965):820.

32. Friedan, 276.

33. Wyden, 77.

34. Evelyn Hooker, "Parental Relations and Male Homosexuality in Patient and Nonpatient Samples," *Journal of Consulting and Clinical Psychology* 33, no. 2 (1969):141.

35. Marvin Siegelman, "Parental Backgrounds of Homo-sexual and Heterosexual Women: A Cross-National Replica-tion," *Archives of Sexual Behavior* 10, no. 4 (1981):372 and other studies by Dr. Siegelman cited there.

36. Bell, Weinberg, and Hammersmith, 183–184, 219.

37. Mary V. Borhek, *Coming Out to Parents, A Two-way Survival Guide for Lesbians and Gay Men and Their Parents* (New York: Pilgrim Press, 1983), 27. (In fact, Borhek's rejection of her guilt feelings is indicated toward the end of *My Son Eric* although not so clearly or definitely stated as in her second book.)

38. Kinsey, Pomeroy, and Martin, 638.

Chapter 10. Them and Us

1. Bruce Voeller, "Society and the Gay Movement," in *Homosexual Behavior, A Modern Reappraisal,* ed. Judd Marmor (New York: Basic Books, 1980), 239.

Chapter 11. Making It Work

1. Ann Greene, Interview with author, Chicago, Illinois, 14 Dec. 1983.

2. Greene, 14 Dec. 1983.

3. T. H. Sauerman, *Read This Before Coming Out to Your Parents,* 1984, 5. (To order this free pamphlet see information in Resources list.)

* * * * *

APPENDIX A

The following graphs and tables visualize the information presented in chapters 4, 5, 7, and 8. The pie graphs may be read horizontally to compare the parents of daughters to the parents of sons. They may also be read vertically to compare parents of both daughters and sons within the two sides of each factor.

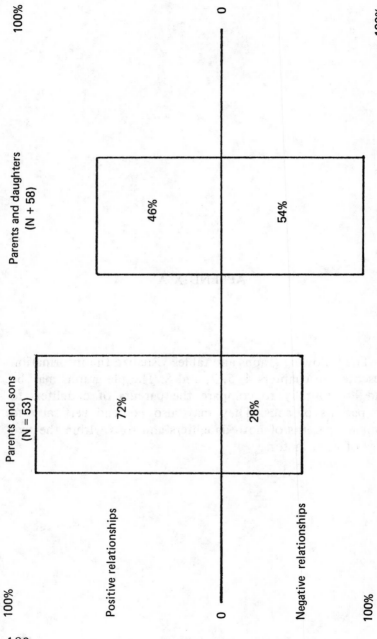

Figure 4-1. Parents and gay sons had more positive relationships than parents and lesbian daughters.

Table 4-1. Four Kinds of Relationships Developed After Disclosures

	Average time since disclosures	% Total relationships (N =111)	% Parent-daughter (N = 58)	% Parent-son (N = 53)
Positive Relationships				
Loving Open Positive interaction between parents, offspring, offspring's friends and lover. Parents open and positive about offspring's sexual orientation to extended family, friends, or others.	5.2 years	11	5	17
Loving Denial Positive contact maintained by parents and offspring. Frequently included lover, but parents otherwise remained closeted with disclosure information. Offspring usually satisfied with parents' level of acceptance.	5.4 years	48	42	55
Negative Relationships				
Resentful Denial Contact maintained but limited by parents' negative view of offspring's sexual orientation. Parents remained closeted.	6.4 years	36	48	23
Hostile Recognition All relationships in this group ended in estrangement. Parents' hostility focused on offspring's sexual orientation.	7.8 years	5	5	5
Totals		100%	100%	100%

181

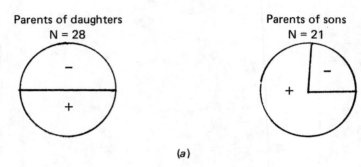

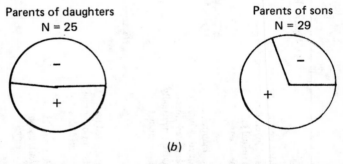

Figure 5-1. Distribution of percentage of positive and negative relationships (*a*) when parents had always attended religious services regularly and (*b*) when parents attended irregularly.

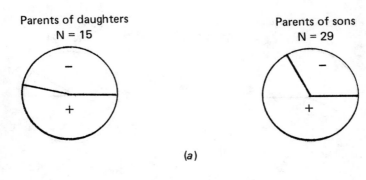

Parents of daughters
N = 15

Parents of sons
N = 29

(a)

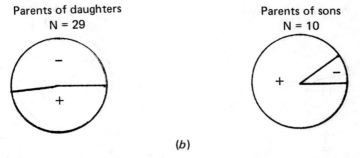

Parents of daughters
N = 29

Parents of sons
N = 10

(b)

Figure 5-2. Distribution of percentage of positive and negative relationships (a) when parents were affiliated with the Roman Catholic Church and (b) when parents were affiliated with a major protestant denomination.

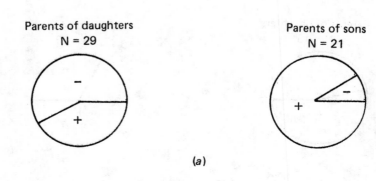

Parents of daughters
N = 29

Parents of sons
N = 21

(a)

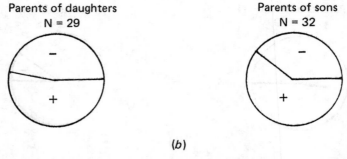

Parents of daughters
N = 29

Parents of sons
N = 32

(b)

Figure 5-3. Distribution of percentage of positive and negative relationships (a) when parents had more than a high school education and (b) when parents had only a high school education or less.

184

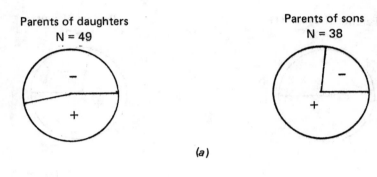

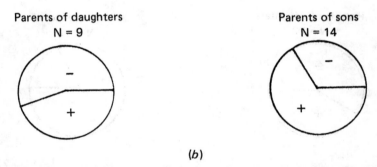

Figure 5-4. Distribution of percentage of positive and negative relationships (*a*) when parents grew up in the U.S. Midwest or South and (*b*) when parents grew up somewhere other than the U.S. Midwest or South.

185

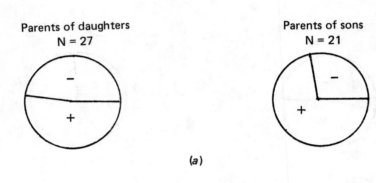

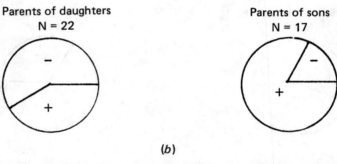

Figure 5-5. Distribution of percentage of positive and negative relationships (a) when parents grew up in Midwestern or Southern cities of more than 250,000 population and (b) when parents grew up in smaller towns or rural areas in the Midwest/South.

Parents of daughters
N = 41

Parents of sons
N = 23

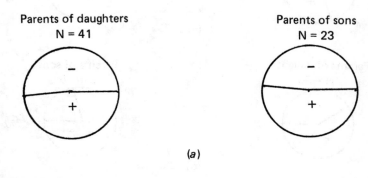

(a)

Parents of daughters
N = 17

Parents of sons
N = 30

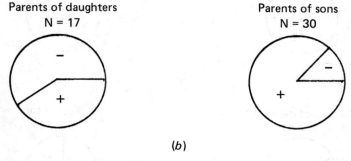

(b)

Figure 5-6. Distribution of percentage of positive and negative relationships (a) when parents were 50 years of age or older at the time of the disclosure and (b) when parents were younger than 50 years.

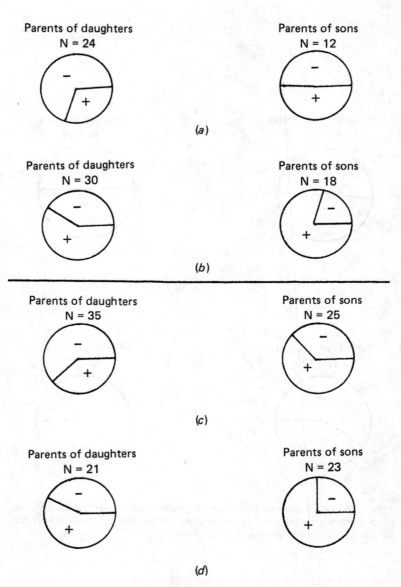

Figure 5-7. Distribution of percentage of positive and negative relationships (*a*) when parents had high or moderate levels of prejudice, (*b*) when parents had low levels of prejudice, (*c*) when parents were politically independent or conservative and (*d*) when parents were politically liberal.

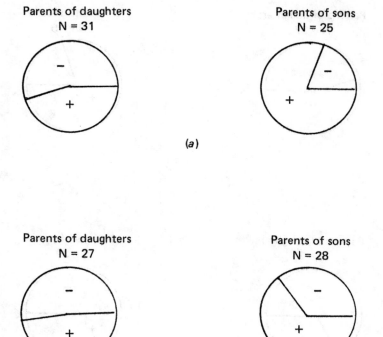

Parents of daughters
N = 31

Parents of sons
N = 25

(a)

Parents of daughters
N = 27

Parents of sons
N = 28

(b)

Figure 5-8. Distribution of percentage of positive and negative relationships (a) when five or more years had elapsed since the disclosure and (b) when less than five years had elapsed.

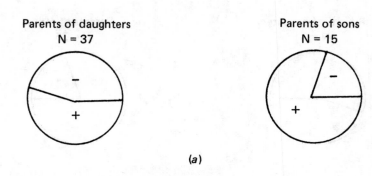

Parents of daughters
N = 37

Parents of sons
N = 15

(a)

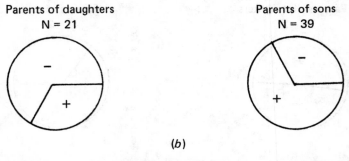

Parents of daughters
N = 21

Parents of sons
N = 39

(b)

Figure 5-9. Distribution of percentage of positive and negative relationships (a) when the daughters and sons were 22 years of age or older at the time of the disclosure and (b) when they were younger than 22.

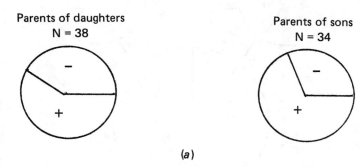

(a)

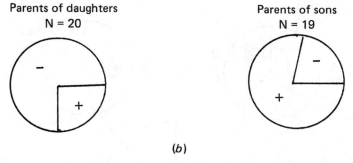

(b)

Figure 5-10. Distribution of percentage of positive and negative relationships (a) when the daughters and sons had two or more siblings and (b) when they had only one or no siblings.

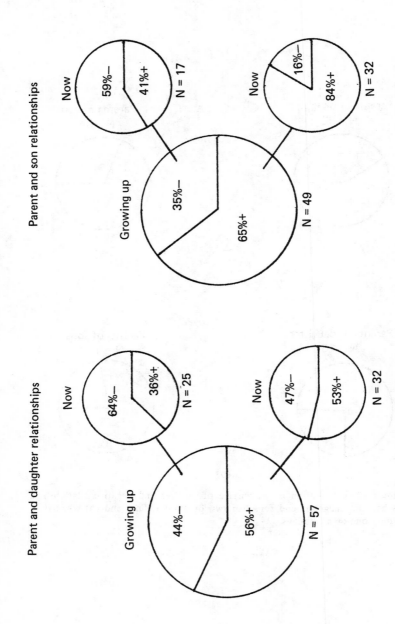

Figure 5-11. Relationships with parents before and after coming out. *Note:* N differs from N in Figure 4-1 because of missing information.

Table 5-1. Distribution of Positive Parent-Daughter Relationships in Factors

Factors	% Positive
Parent with low prejudice level	60
Daughter with 2 or more siblings	58
Politically liberal parent	57
Daughter age 22 or older at disclosure	54
Daughter who felt appreciated and approved while growing up	53
Roman Catholic parent	53
Parent who attended church irregularly	52
Parent from city of 250,000+ population in Midwest or South U.S.	52
Parent with high school education or less	52
Parent who always attended church regularly	50
Parent age 50 or older at disclosure	49
Less than 5 years since disclosure	48
Parent affiliated with a major protestant denomination	48
Parent from U.S. Midwest or South	47
Five or more years since disclosure	45
Parent from somewhere other than Midwest or South	44
Parent from small town or rural area in Midwest or South	41
Parent with high school+ education	41
Parent younger than 50 at disclosure	41
Politically conservative parent	37
Daughter who did not feel appreciated and approved while growing up	36
Daughter younger than 22 at disclosure	33
Parent with high or moderate prejudice level	29
Daughter with 1 or no siblings	25

Table 5-2. Distribution of Positive Parent-Son Relationships in Factors

Factors	% Positive
Parent with high school+ education	90
Parent affiliated with a major protestant denomination	90
Parent younger than 50 at disclosure	87
Son who felt appreciated and approved while growing up	84
Parent from small town or rural area in Midwest or South	82
Five or more years since disclosure	80
Son age 22 or older at disclosure	80
Son with 1 or no siblings	79
Parent with low prejudice level	78
Parent from U.S. Midwest or South	76
Parent who always attended church regularly	76
Politically liberal parent	74
Parent from city of 250,000+ population in Midwest or South U.S.	71
Parent who attended church irregularly	69
Son with 2 or more siblings	68
Son younger than 22 at disclosure	67
Roman Catholic parent	66
Parent from somewhere other than Midwest or South	64
Less than 5 years since disclosure	64
Politically conservative parent	64
Parent with high school education or less	59
Parent age 50 or older at disclosure	52
Parent with high or moderate prejudice level	50
Son who did not feel appreciated and approved while growing up	41

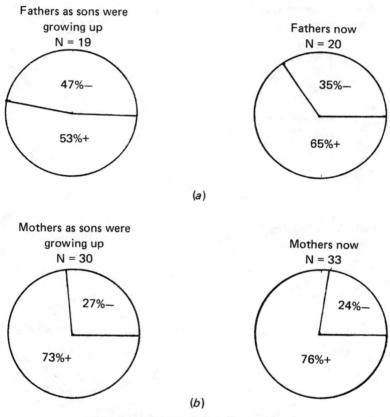

Fathers as sons were
growing up
N = 19

47%−

53%+

Fathers now
N = 20

35%−

65%+

(a)

Mothers as sons were
growing up
N = 30

27%−

73%+

Mothers now
N = 33

24%−

76%+

(b)

Note: N differs because of missing information.

Figure 7-1. Fathers and mothers of sons (*a*) same-sex parent relationships and (*b*) opposite-sex parent relationships.

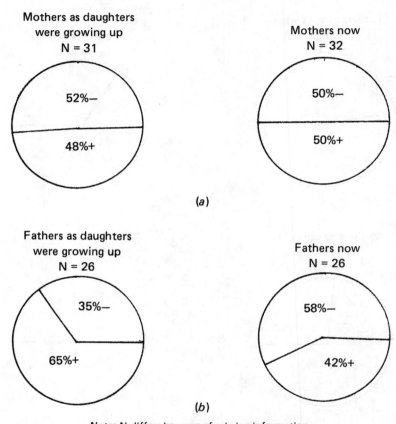

Mothers as daughters
were growing up
N = 31

52%−

48%+

Mothers now
N = 32

50%−

50%+

(a)

Fathers as daughters
were growing up
N = 26

35%−

65%+

Fathers now
N = 26

58%−

42%+

(b)

Note: N differs because of missing information.

Figure 8-1. Mothers and fathers of daughters (*a*) same-sex parent relationships and (*b*) opposite-sex parent relationships.

APPENDIX B

Description of Sample

This book draws equally from the life stories of both women and men. Of the seventy-one people who contributed to the book, 42% were lesbians; 10% were parents of lesbian daughters; 44% were gay men, and 4% were parents of gay sons. Moreover, 17% of the respondents were black, a higher percentage of blacks than are present in the overall population.

In addition, the average age of the daughters was 29 years, and these young women had 3.5 years of education beyond high school. The sons were, on the average, 26 years old with 2.6 years post high school education. Twenty-five percent of the daughters and sons were affiliated with Protestant religious denominations; 24% were Roman Catholics; 10% belonged to the Metropolitan Community

Church; 7% were Jewish; 3% were affiliated with other religions, and 31% had no religious affiliation.

Ninety-three percent of the respondents lived within 150 miles of Chicago, Illinois. About a third were contacted through Chicago's Parents and Friends of Lesbians and Gays, Inc., a support group for parents. The others came through a network of those original contacts and other friends as well as Chicago's Gay Horizon's Youth Group and the Illinois Gay and Lesbian Task Force.

The stories of the respondents were gathered by me through use of the following interview guide which my son Jason helped me construct. Sixty-eight of the interviews were done personally; one son and the parents of one daughter were interviewed through the mail.

* * * * *

Interview Guide

1. How old are you?
2. Are your parents still living? If yes, how old are they? If no, how long ago did they die?
3. Are you an adopted or born child?
4. How many brothers and sisters do you have? Ages and sex?
5. What is your numerical placement in the family?
6. Are any of your brothers and sisters gay that you know of? If yes, how did you learn this?
7. Are your parents divorced? If yes, how old were you at the time and with which parent did you then live?
8. Do you live with your parents now?
9. What is your family's ethnic identification?
10. Where did your parents come from?
11. Where did you grow up?

12. What is your religious affiliation? Do you attend religious services regularly?

13. What is your parents' religious affiliation? Do they attend regularly? Did they attend regularly as you were growing up?

14. What is your educational background?

15. What are the educational backgrounds of your parents?

16. What is your mother's occupation? Dad's?

17. Were your parents politicallly conservative (generally this means Republican) or liberal (Democratic) as you were growing up?

18. Do you have an idea how your folks felt about blacks or other groups different from themselves as you were growing up?

19. Gay people?

20. Did you talk openly about sex at home as you were growing up?

21. What kind of person do you think your folks thought you were as you were growing up?

22. What was their dream for you?

23. Did your folks show affection towards you as you were growing up?

24. Was one parent more affectionate than the other?

25. Did either of them suspect you were gay/lesbian?

26. How did your parents respond to you during these different times in your life:

    A. From birth till age 7?

        1. by showing appreciation and approval openly with words and actions?

        2. by showing appreciation and approval privately, not openly?

        3. by showing appreciation and approval unevenly, so you were never sure what to expect?

        4. by withholding appreciation and approval all or most of the time?

    B. From age 7 till about 14 or puberty?

    C. From age 14 to 21?

27. Do both your mother and father know that you are a gay man or a lesbian?

28. How long has it been since each of them became aware?

29. How old were you when each of them became aware?

30. Was your coming out to them an accident or did you plan it?

31. Had you tried to prepare yourself for coming out to your parents? How?

32. Had your tried to prepare your folks? How?

33. Please describe the physical place where you all were the day you came out to your folks.

34. Were you alone with them?

35. Do you remember how you felt about yourself as a gay person on the day you told them?

36. Please describe how the disclosure happened.

37. Do you remember the exact words you used?

38. Do you remember anything else about the disclosure?

39. Please describe your parents' immediate reaction.

40. Did they both react in the same way? If not, how did each react?

41. What did each of them say?

42. How did they act, what were their physical movements?

43. Did they react the way you expected? If not, what had you expected?

44. Did one or the other of them seem to lead the initial reaction? If so, which one?

45. Do you wish you hadn't told them or that they hadn't found out?

46. Do you wish you'd told them or they'd found out at a different time or in a different way?

47. Does it seem to you that your parents went through different stages of reaction?

48. After the initial reaction, how did they act?
49. Are they more accepting now than they were the day you told them?
50. Can you give an example of their greater/lesser acceptance?
51. Do you think they're still reacting or have they pretty much settled on how they feel about it?
52. Do you think your parents take responsibility for your gayness?
53. Have your parents told your brothers, sisters, relatives, friends that you're gay?
54. Do you and your folks talk about the people or the events in your life that identify you as a gay person?
55. Are you comfortable talking to your folks about these parts of your life?
56. Do you have conversations about these subjects very often?
57. Are you free to bring gay friends to your parents' home?
58. Are you free to bring lovers to your parents' home?
59. Did the quality of your relationship with your mother/father change after they came to know you were gay?
60. Was the change for better or for worse? Can you give examples?
61. Has their knowing increased or decreased *your* feelings of closeness to them? Please explain.
62. Try to evaluate the quality of your present relationship as a lesbian/gay man with your mother/father. Give each relationship a number between 1 and 4 where:
    1 is acceptance and approval
    2 is acceptance but not approval
    3 is conditional acceptance
    4 is unacceptance or rejection.

63. Do you expect your mother/father to become more accepting or even affirming of you in the future?
64. If so, what do you think might cause that to happen?
65. If not, what kind of experience or event can you imagine that might cause them to become more accepting?
66. What is the best possible relationship you could have with your folks? What would make you the most happy?
67. How do you think your parents would react if the President and First Lady called a press conference to say that their son was a gay man and they not only love him but think having a gay son has enriched their lives?
68. What advice would you have for someone else who is thinking of coming out to her or his parents?

Note: Parents who were interviewed were asked almost exactly the same questions about their relationships with their daughters or sons.

* * * * *

Understanding Stories as Relationships

Each interview transcript was carefully read and notated on three forms. Form 1 was a fact sheet of demographic information, details of each disclosure, and a summary of parents' reactions to the disclosures. Form 2, an example sheet, served as an index to locate specific information in each transcript.

The third form, called Reactions, synthesized the events that followed the disclosure in each family. It identified five categories of parents' behavior and provided space to identify the daughter's or son's response to those behaviors.

The five categories were: Emotional, Hostile/Irrational, Denial/Dishonest, Intellectual, and Loving/Open. A list of examples followed each category heading. For instance, Hid Feelings, Wouldn't Discuss, and Expressed Change Wish appeared under the heading Denial/Dishonest. Different color inks were used to differentiate between parents' initial response, defined as what happened in the first few days after the disclosure, and what happened later. The actions of mothers and fathers were notated separately as were the child's responses.

In a few stories, the family's interaction changed abruptly after several years had passed. One family, for example, began to communicate in very different ways after both the mother and son encountered life-threatening experiences. Those examples were distinguished by a third color ink.

The stories, of course, varied in length and amount of detail; some filled more than one set of forms. But, unexpectedly, Form 3 presented a visual picture that was not wholly reliant on the respondent's verbal skills in that the number of examples became less important than the examples themselves. To illustrate, one daughter remembered over a dozen remarks her parents had made during the three and a half years that followed the disclosure. All of the remarks demonstrated denial: "Don't tell us those things,"; "Don't tell your friends"; "This wouldn't have happened if you hadn't moved to Chicago"; "Graduate school must have done it"; "This woman has done it to you," and so on. In contrast, a son used only three examples to describe the same thing. After four years, he said, his mother "still talks in stilted language, avoids facing who I am, and occasionally suggests that since I haven't been in a relationship for two years that this would be a good time for me to go out and find a woman."

When all the examples were notated, individual families

could be compared, and several things became apparent. First, the different colored inks showed that most of the notations under the Emotional heading described events that had occurred at the time of the disclosure or shortly thereafter. Thus, it seemed, logically enough, that most parents were more emotional at first than they were later. As a result of that observation, the notations in the Emotional category were separated from the others and used to formulate the material on initial reactions that was presented in Chapter 3.

Second, certain patterns appeared in the remaining notations.

- The notations under Hostile/Irrational and Loving/ Open were mutually exclusive. In other words, those two categories represented the opposite extremes of parents' responses, and only one parent had displayed both.
- The actions of most parents appeared clustered under two or three categories. Entire categories remained blank on many forms. In fact, only one story distributed itself evenly across all the categories.
- Most parents' actions illustrated some form of denial.
- Parents set the tone of the relationships while daughters and sons were generally passive observers of their parents' reactions.

From those patterns, four different types of relationships, as set out in Chapter 4, were identified: Hostile Recognition; Resentful Denial; Loving Denial; and Loving Open. The four relationships are further defined in Table 4-1 of Appendix A.

* * * * *

FORM 1

Fact Sheet Tr #_____ Black/White Son/Dgtr/M/F of _____

Present ages: Child _____ M/F _____ C/O ages: Child_____ M/F _____

Time elapsed between c/o and interview _____

Ethnicity: M _____ F_____

Grew up: M _____ F_____ Child _____

Education: M _____ F_____ Child _____

Prejudice Black/White: M _____ F _____

Prejudice Gay: M_____ F _____

Sex discussions_____

Politics: M _____ F _____

Religion, Growing up: M _____ F _____

        Present: M _____ F _____

Suspicions: Who?_____ Why? _____ When? _____

Disclosure

Place _____ Accident/Plan

Who present _____

Who initiated _____

Catalyst _____

Words _____

Method _____

Preparation _____

Reaction Summary

Capsule reaction _____
_____

Mother versus father: _____
_____

Initial reaction versus later behavior_____
_____

Comments _____
_____

205

FORM 2

Examples Tr # _____   Black/White   Son/Dgtr/M/F of _____

Sex Roles

Mother: child-centered _____

work-centered _____

martyr _____

dictator _____

other _____

Father: silent _____

_____

other _____

_____

Traditional family _____

Nontraditional parent _____

Reactions

Leap of love _____

Gay sibling/relative _____

Pregnant daughter _____

Other previous coping _____

X-gender/clothing/appearance _____

Reading _____

Fears _____

To lover/changes in child's life _____

Siblings' reactions _____

Tacit Recognition

Life Changes/Benefits to Parent

Values, Carried Over or Not

Helping Professions: Child/Parent

Other

206

Form 3

Reactions Tr # ___ Black/White   Son/Dgtr/M/F of _____
Time lapse between disclosure and interview_____

Mother   Father

Emotional

Tears _____
Disappointment _____
Other _____
Child's response _____

Hostile/Irrational

Remarks _____
Death wish _____
Emotional rejection _____
Financial rejection _____
Physical acts _____
Other _____
Child's response _____

Denial/Dishonest

No reaction _____
Hid feelings _____
Wouldn't discuss _____
Warnings _____
Blame _____
Change wish _____
Other _____
Child's response _____

Intellectual

Questions _____
Advice _____
Other _____
Child's response _____

Loving/Open

Physical _____
Verbal _____
Openness _____
Other _____
Child's response _____

Time frame/other comments: _____
_____

INDEX

A few of the publications of
THE NAIAD PRESS, INC.
P.O. Box 10543 • Tallahassee, Florida 32302
Phone (904) 539-9322
Mail orders welcome. Please include 15% postage.

PARENTS MATTER by Ann Muller. 240 pp. Parents' relationships with lesbian daughters and gay sons.
ISBN 0-930044-91-6 $9.95

THE PEARLS by Shelley Smith. 176 pp. Passion and fun in the Caribbean sun.   ISBN 0-930044-93-2 $7.95

MAGDALENA by Sarah Aldridge. 352 pp. Epic Lesbian novel set on three continents.   ISBN 0-930044-99-1 $8.95

THE BLACK AND WHITE OF IT by Ann Allen Shockley. 144 pp. Short stories.   ISBN 0-930044-96-7 $7.95

SAY JESUS AND COME TO ME by Ann Allen Shockley. 288 pp. Contemporary romance.   ISBN 0-930044-98-3   8.95

LOVING HER by Ann Allen Shockley. 192 pp. Romantic love story.   ISBN 0-930044-97-5   7.95

MURDER AT THE NIGHTWOOD BAR by Katherine V. Forrest. 240 pp. A Kate Delafield mystery. Second in a series.
ISBN 0-930044-92-4   8.95

ZOE'S BOOK by Gail Pass. 224 pp. Passionate, obsessive love story.   ISBN 0-930044-95-9   7.95

WINGED DANCER by Camarin Grae. 228 pp. Erotic Lesbian adventure story.   ISBN 0-930044-88-6   8.95

PAZ by Camarin Grae. 336 pp. Romantic Lesbian adventurer with the power to change the world.   ISBN 0-930044-89-4   8.95

SOUL SNATCHER by Camarin Grae. 224 pp. A puzzle, an adventure, a mystery—Lesbian romance.   ISBN 0-930044-90-8   8.95

THE LOVE OF GOOD WOMEN by Isabel Miller. 224 pp. Long-awaited new novel by the author of the beloved *Patience and Sarah*.   ISBN 0-930044-81-9   8.95

THE HOUSE AT PELHAM FALLS by Brenda Weathers. 240 pp. Suspenseful Lesbian ghost story.   ISBN 0-930044-79-7   7.95

HOME IN YOUR HANDS by Lee Lynch. 240 pp. More stories from the author of *Old Dyke Tales*.   ISBN 0-930044-80-0   7.95

EACH HAND A MAP by Anita Skeen. 112 pp. Real-life poems that touch us all.   ISBN 0-930044-82-7   6.95

SURPLUS by Sylvia Stevenson. 342 pp. A classic early Lesbian novel.   ISBN 0-930044-78-9   7.95

PEMBROKE PARK by Michelle Martin. 256 pp. Derring-do and daring romance in Regency England. ISBN 0-930044-77-0   7.95

THE LONG TRAIL by Penny Hayes. 248 pp. Vivid adventures of two women in love in the old west.   ISBN 0-930044-76-2   8.95

HORIZON OF THE HEART by Shelley Smith. 192 pp. Hot romance in summertime New England.   ISBN 0-930044-75-4   7.95

TOOTHPICK HOUSE by Lee Lynch. 264 pp. Love between
two Lesbians of different classes.   ISBN 0-930044-45-2   7.95

MADAME AURORA by Sarah Aldridge. 256 pp. Historical
novel featuring a charismatic "seer."   ISBN 0-930044-44-4   7.95

CURIOUS WINE by Katherine V. Forrest. 176 pp. Passionate
Lesbian love story, a best-seller.   ISBN 0-930044-43-6   7.95

BLACK LESBIAN IN WHITE AMERICA by Anita Cornwell.
141 pp. Stories, essays, autobiography.   ISBN 0-930044-41-X   7.50

CONTRACT WITH THE WORLD by Jane Rule. 340 pp.
Powerful, panoramic novel of gay life.   ISBN 0-930044-28-2   7.95

YANTRAS OF WOMANLOVE by Tee A. Corinne. 64 pp.
Photos by noted Lesbian photographer.   ISBN 0-930044-30-4   6.95

MRS. PORTER'S LETTER by Vicki P. McConnell. 224 pp.
The first Nyla Wade mystery.   ISBN 0-930044-29-0   7.95

TO THE CLEVELAND STATION by Carol Anne Douglas.
192 pp. Interracial Lesbian love story.   ISBN 0-930044-27-4   6.95

THE NESTING PLACE by Sarah Aldridge. 224 pp. Historical
novel, a three-woman triangle.   ISBN 0-930044-26-6   7.95

THIS IS NOT FOR YOU by Jane Rule. 284 pp. A letter to a
beloved is also an intricate novel.   ISBN 0-930044-25-8   7.95

FAULTLINE by Sheila Ortiz Taylor. 140 pp. Warm, funny,
literate story of a startling family.   ISBN 0-930044-24-X   6.95

THE LESBIAN IN LITERATURE by Barbara Grier. 3d ed.
Foreword by Maida Tilchen. 240 pp. Comprehensive bibliography. Literary ratings; rare photos.   ISBN 0-930044-23-1   7.95

ANNA'S COUNTRY by Elizabeth Lang. 208 pp. A woman
finds her Lesbian identity.   ISBN 0-930044-19-3   6.95

PRISM by Valerie Taylor. 158 pp. A love affair between two
women in their sixties.   ISBN 0-930044-18-5   6.95

BLACK LESBIANS: AN ANNOTATED BIBLIOGRAPHY
compiled by J.R. Roberts. Foreword by Barbara Smith. 112
pp. Award winning bibliography.   ISBN 0-930044-21-5   5.95

THE MARQUISE AND THE NOVICE by Victoria Ramstetter.
108 pp. A Lesbian Gothic novel.   ISBN 0-930044-16-9   4.95

OUTLANDER by Jane Rule. 207 pp. Short stories and essays
by one of our finest writers.   ISBN 0-930044-17-7   6.95

SAPPHISTRY: THE BOOK OF LESBIAN SEXUALITY by
Pat Califia. 2d edition, revised. 195 pp.   ISBN 0-930044-47-9   7.95

ALL TRUE LOVERS by Sarah Aldridge. 292 pp. Romantic
novel set in the 1930s and 1940s.   ISBN 0-930044-10-X   7.95

A WOMAN APPEARED TO ME by Renee Vivien. 65 pp. A
classic; translated by Jeannette H. Foster. ISBN 0-930044-06-1   5.00

CYTHEREA'S BREATH by Sarah Aldridge. 240 pp. Women
first enter medicine and the law: a novel. ISBN 0-930044-02-9   6.95

TOTTIE by Sarah Aldridge. 181 pp. Lesbian romance in the
turmoil of the sixties.   ISBN 0-930044-01-0   6.95

THE LATECOMER by Sarah Aldridge. 107 pp. A delicate love
story set in days gone by.   ISBN 0-930044-00-2   5.00

ODD GIRL OUT by Ann Bannon   ISBN 0-930044-83-5   5.95
I AM A WOMAN by Ann Bannon.   ISBN 0-930044-84-3   5.95
WOMEN IN THE SHADOWS by Ann Bannon.
                      ISBN 0-930044-85-1   5.95
JOURNEY TO A WOMAN by Ann Bannon.
                      ISBN 0-930044-86-X   5.95
BEEBO BRINKER by Ann Bannon   ISBN 0-930044-87-8   5.95
   Legendary novels written in the fifties and sixties,
     set in the gay mecca of Greenwich Village.

VOLUTE BOOKS

JOURNEY TO FULFILLMENT   Early classics by Valerie   3.95
A WORLD WITHOUT MEN   Taylor: The Erika Frohmann   3.95
RETURN TO LESBOS   series.   3.95

These are just a few of the many Naiad Press titles—we are the oldest
and largest lesbian/feminist publishing company in the world. Please
request a complete catalog. We offer personal service; we encourage and
welcome direct mail orders from individuals who have limited access to
bookstores carrying our publications.